D1180306

The Observer's Pocket Series

BRITISH AWARDS AND MEDALS

The Observer Books

A POCKET REFERENCE SERIES COVERING
A WIDE RANGE OF SUBJECTS

The Observer's Book of

BRITISH AWARDS AND MEDALS

EDWARD C. JOSLIN

WITH 186 BLACK AND WHITE

ILLUSTRATIONS AND 8 PAGES

OF COLOUR ILLUSTRATIONS

FREDERICK WARNE & CO LTD
FREDERICK WARNE & CO INC
LONDON : NEW YORK

*THE SIX COLOUR PLATES OF
MEDAL RIBBONS WERE DRAWN
BY MICHAEL TREGENZA*

LIBRARY OF CONGRESS CATALOG
CARD NO. 74–80608

ISBN 0 7232 1538 3

*Printed in Great Britain by
William Clowes & Sons, Limited
London, Beccles and Colchester
8.774*

CONTENTS

LIST OF COLOUR PLATES

PREFACE

There comes a time when man, whether he be a young student or possibly a senior citizen, retiring from the rush and turmoil of a busy day, desires to have his mind diverted from the pressures of his business or professional calling. He looks for recreation in something which will exercise the mind, create its own restful pleasure and be of such a nature as will enable him also to entertain his friends and colleagues.

There is perhaps nothing more entertaining—yet less expensive than many forms of collecting—than the formation of a collection of Orders, Decorations or Medals, which represent our Island's proud heritage of naval and military achievements during the last two hundred years. Orders, Decorations and Medals are the official and tangible tokens of recognition awarded by the Sovereign or Government for services to the country. These relics help to recall a particular war, campaign, or action, and to keep alive the service of a particular officer, man or regiment, or perhaps some outstanding act of gallantry which, with our diminishing armed forces, serve as a constant reminder of the outstanding yet often forgotten deeds of our ancestors. To mention a few:

Nelson's defeat of the French at the Battle of the Nile, thus saving Egypt and, indirectly, India, from French conquest.

Nelson's overwhelming defeat of the combined French and Spanish fleets at Trafalgar, which finally ruled out Napoleon's invasion of these islands.

The masterly retreat and evacuation at Corunna in 1809 under the leadership of General Sir John Moore.

Wellington's brilliant victories over the previously all-victorious French army in Spain and Portugal from 1809–14.

The immortal Charge of the Light Brigade at Balaclava.

The heroic defence of Rorke's Drift 1877–9 whilst surrounded by an overwhelming force of Zulu warriors; and more recently,

The Retreat to Mons by the 'contemptible little army' in the face of overwhelming German superiority; and, of course, countless other actions fought in all corners of the globe.

The collecting of medals, the issue of which in Great Britain and the Commonwealth has always been restricted to the actual participants, has been carried on for a hundred years or so, but only in recent years have we seen much increased activity in this particular field.

My aim in writing this volume is to provide the student and 'young' collector with a ready 'pocket' reference to aid recognition of the fascinating series of British Orders, Decorations and Medals. Owing to the fact that their issue and manufacture has always been severely restricted, they are very collectable. However, being written as an introduction only or as a 'first' course, what does the collector look for when considering his 'second or main' course? From here onwards he should expect to purchase one or more of the undermentioned:

* *British Battles and Medals* by Major L. L. Gordon, 4th edition revised by E. C. Joslin, published by Spink & Son Ltd.
* *The Standard Catalogue of British Orders Decorations*

and Medals by E. C. Joslin, published by Spink & Son Ltd.

Ribbons and Medals by Captain H. Taprell Dorling, published by George Philip & Son Ltd.

British Gallantry Awards by P. E. Abbott & J. H. A. Tamplin, published by Guinness Superlatives Ltd.

Collecting Medals and Decorations by Alex A. Purves, published by B. A. Seaby Ltd.

all of which are in print, plus numerous others which are only obtainable in the second-hand book market or from a specialist dealer in medals.

The author cannot possibly overlook the debt he owes to the Royal Medallists, Spink & Son Ltd., of London, for their very considerable help in not only providing all the Orders, Decorations and Medals for the illustrations, but also in allowing passages to be quoted from their publications*.

In conclusion it gives me great personal satisfaction to gratefully acknowledge the help and guidance that David Spink, the doyen of medallists and my mentor, has given me with my publications since I first joined his company nearly thirty years ago.

EDWARD C. JOSLIN

1 ORDER OF THE GARTER
(a) (*left*) Sash badge (b) (*right*) Star

2 ORDER OF THE THISTLE
(a) (*left*) Star (b) (*right*) Sash badge

ORDERS OF KNIGHTHOOD

The Most Noble Order of the Garter, founded by King Edward III, is the premier Order of Great Britain and as such commands the very highest respect. The Order, which is the personal gift of the Sovereign, consists of 25 Knights only and, consequently, is one of the rarest Orders in existence today. Furthermore, unlike some other Orders it has never been in a state of suspended animation as it has been awarded continuously since the middle of the 14th century. The insignia consists of a sky-blue riband worn over the *left* shoulder from which is suspended an oval gold pierced badge known as 'The Lesser George'. A silver eight-pointed star with a gold and enamel centre is worn on the left breast. On important state occasions a gold and enamel collar chain is worn around the neck from which is suspended 'the Great George', this being a three-dimensional equestrian figure of St George slaying a dragon. The motto of the Order is 'HONI SOIT QUI MAL Y PENSE' or 'Evil be who evil thinks'.

The 25 Knights comprise selected Christian heads of state, distinguished military leaders, politicians, and civilians who have rendered exceptional services. In addition, a small number of 'extra' Knights are admitted such as three successive Emperors of Japan and two Sultans of Turkey. Sir Winston Churchill is probably the most outstanding commoner to be awarded the Order in recent years and it is interesting to note that he was invested with the insignia worn by one of his forbears, the 1st Duke of Marlborough, who was admitted to the Order in 1702.

2 **The Most Ancient and Most Noble Order of the Thistle** The generally accepted date of foundation is 1687, and the Order was revived by Queen Anne in 1703. Although it is suggested that the Order was founded as far back as 787, this is thought to be a legend. If it were true, and some believe it is, then it might be said to be senior to the Garter, and claims of this nature have been made. The insignia comprises a dark green riband worn over the *left* shoulder, from which is suspended a badge depicting St Andrew bearing a cross, surrounded by the motto. The breast star embraces the cross of St Andrew with rays in the angles, the centre contains an enamelled thistle surrounded by 'NEMO ME IMPUNE LACESSIT' or 'No one provokes me with impunity'. As with all British Orders, a collar chain is included in the insignia which is in gold and enamel, with alternate devices of thistles and sprigs of rue, these being ancient symbols of the Picts and Scots.

The Order is restricted to 16 distinguished Scotsmen (thus making it more exclusive than the Garter and probably the rarest in Europe) and as occasion demands, extra Knights who are selected members of the Royal Family. No foreigner had been made a Knight for over 200 years until King Olav was admitted as an extra Knight in 1962. It is not awarded to non-Christians.

3 **The Most Illustrious Order of St Patrick** Unlike the other two Great Orders, i.e. the Garter, and Thistle, the date that the St Patrick was instituted or founded cannot be questioned, this being 1783. Originally founded as a gesture of goodwill towards Ireland, it was made available to Irish peers who had rendered distinguished services and to those who could not be admitted to the Order of the Garter. The Order was restricted in 1833 to 22 Knights. The insignia is particularly decorative; the sash riband worn over the *left* shoulder is sky-blue in colour, with an oval pierced badge suspended from it. This consists of a shamrock

3 ORDER OF ST PATRICK
(a) (*left*) Star (b) (*right*) Sash badge

with three crowns on its leaves, the shamrock being placed on a cross of St Patrick. The centre is surrounded by an oval bearing the legend 'QUIS SEPARABIT'—'Who shall separate'—and the date, 'MDCCLXXXIII'. The gold and enamel collar chain consists of alternate roses and harps. The breast star is of silver with a representation of the sash badge in the centre. The Order was discontinued after the formation of the Irish Republic in 1922; the last holder of the K.P. was H.R.H. The late Duke of Gloucester who died in 1974.

During the Second World War a number of distinguished service leaders, whose families were associated with Northern Ireland, would probably have qualified as Knights. Although it was suggested that the Order be kept alive by such appointments, the separation of the North and South of Ireland made the revival impractical.

4 **The Most Honourable Order of the Bath** Originally founded in 1725 during the time of the Prime Minister, Sir Robert Walpole. It was an Order with one class and one division, the recipients being known as K.B.s., or simply Knights of the Bath. The title was derived from the ancient ritual of bathing or cleaning (since discontinued) which was symbolical of washing away impurities before admission to the Order. In 1815, following the successful conclusion of the Napoleonic Wars, the Prince Regent (later George IV) found it necessary to reward distinguished officers of the two services. Consequently two divisions were formed: the civil, which retained the original design of insignia and maintained a single class, and a military division which consisted of three classes. These were G.C.B. (Knight Grand Cross), K.C.B. (Knight Commander) and C.B. (Companion of the Bath).

However, in 1847 it was found necessary also to enlarge the civil division to three classes to correspond with the military division. Admission to the Order is still granted sparingly. Consequently it is probably the most highly regarded of all the 'lesser' orders. The motto of the Order is 'TRIA JUNCTA IN UNO', 'Three joined in one', (England, Scotland and Ireland).

5 **The Order of Merit** is one of the most coveted of British distinctions. It was introduced by King Edward VII in 1902 as a very special distinction to those supreme in the fields of art, music and literature, and is also occasionally awarded to military leaders in time of war.

The Order is limited to 24 members and also a limited number of foreign recipients. As with the Victorian Order, the Order of Merit is the gift of the Sovereign, but it carries no rank apart from the initials 'O.M.' after the name. This distinction is also awarded to ladies, but the only one granted to date has been to Florence Nightingale. Other well-known public figures given

4 ORDER OF THE BATH
(a) (*left*) Sash
badge, military
division

4 (b) (*above*) Neck
badge, civil division

5 ORDER OF MERIT
(*left*) Badge, military
division

this honour were Sir Winston Churchill and General Eisenhower (later President of the U.S.A.).

The insignia consists of a gold and enamel badge in the form of a crowned cross. Military recipients have crossed swords added which pass through the centre. The riband is half blue, half red, being the same shades as the Garter and Bath.

6 The Royal Guelphic Order Instituted in 1815 by the Prince Regent and awarded by the Crown of Hanover to Service men and civilians for distinguished services; this award was given to both British and Hanoverian subjects. However, by the Law of Hanover a woman could not ascend the throne. Consequently, after the death of William IV, Queen Victoria could not adopt the title of Sovereign and the Duke of Cumberland, fifth son of George III, became King of Hanover. From then on the Guelphic Order became a totally Hanoverian award. As with the Order of the Bath which the insignia resembled, it comprised three

6 GUELPHIC ORDER
(a) (*left*) Sash badge, civil division
6 (b) (*above*) Star, military division 1st class

classes with both military and civilian divisions. The motto of the Order is 'NEC ASPERA TERRENT', 'Difficulties do not terrify'.

The main recipients, especially in the 1815 period, were distinguished British and Hanoverian Officers who fought Napoleon, many Hanoverian regiments having fought with distinction under Wellington in the Peninsular War and at Waterloo.

The Most Exalted Order of the Star of India 7

Founded in 1861 as a reward for services in connection with India. After the Mutiny of 1857–8, the British Crown took over the administration of the Indian subcontinent from the private trading company known as the Honourable East India Company. Then it was found necessary to have an Order as a mark of the British Government's esteem for the loyal Princes and others. The insignia, especially the G.C.S.I., namely the 1st class or Knight Grand Commander, is the most

7 STAR OF INDIA
(a) (*left*) Sash badge   (b) (*above*)
Star, 1st class

magnificent of all British Orders. As it was awarded to the Viceroy and Indian Princes, it was of gold and enamel set with diamonds.

The insignia of the Order has always been returnable to the Central Chancery on death, but recipients or their families were, for a time, allowed to purchase the insignia after the Order was discontinued in 1947.

The motto of the Order is particularly apt—'HEAVENS LIGHT OUR GUIDE' being acceptable to all religions. The Order consisted of three classes: the G.C.S.I. as already mentioned, the K.C.S.I.—Knight Commander, and the C.S.I.—Companion.

8 The Most Distinguished Order of St Michael and St George
Founded in 1818 by the Prince Regent as an award of appreciation for services rendered by the population of the Ionian Isles, in the Mediterranean, which in 1815 had been formed as an independent kingdom under the protection of Great Britain. The islands, acquired as a result of the Napoleonic War, were at that time very important strategically. Later on in the 19th century, owing to the growing extent of the British Empire, the Order was made available to those who had rendered distinguished services in the Colonies and in foreign affairs. Hence the motto 'AUSPICIUM MELIORIS ÆVI'—'Token of a better age'.

As with the Order of the Bath, the Order comprises three classes: G.C.M.G. (Knight Grand Cross), K.C.M.G. (Knight Commander) and C.M.G. (Companion). As with all British Orders, the insignia was originally in gold and enamel, but from 1887, for reasons of economy the insignia were reproduced in silver gilt. As with all the British Orders, it is only the 1st and 2nd classes which carry a title of Knighthood. During recent years women have been admitted to the order but their numbers to date are very few.

9 The Most Eminent Order of the Indian Empire
This is the second of the Indian Orders, and it was

8 ST MICHAEL & ST GEORGE
(a) (*left*) Neck badge (b) (*below*) Star, 1st class

9 INDIAN EMPIRE
(a) (*above*) Star (b) (*right*) Neck badge

founded by Queen Victoria in 1878, when she adopted the title Empress of India, hence the motto 'IMPERA-TRICIS AUSPICIIS'—'Under the auspices of the Empress'. The Order was discontinued in 1947 owing to independence being granted to India and Pakistan. Originally founded as a one-class Order, namely Companion, it was extended in 1887 to three classes. This is the fourth and final British Order which has been discontinued owing to political reasons, the others being the Orders of St Patrick, Guelphic and Star of India. As with the Star of India, the basic design of the insignia omitted a cross which would not have been accepted by the non-Christian recipients, and it did not have a patron saint. The Order was intended to serve as a junior Order to the Star of India, a certain proportion being awarded to Officers of the Services.

The third-class badge of all the Orders were, until 1917, worn on the breast in the same way as a medal. Since then they have always been worn around the neck.

10 **The Imperial Order of the Crown of India** was introduced in 1878 as an award to ladies only, for services in connection with India. The Order, which was discontinued in 1947, was awarded to female members of the Royal Family, Indian Princesses and those connected with the Viceroy of India and the Governors of the Provinces.

The Order comprised one class only and did not carry any title or precedence, although membership was very selective indeed. The oval badge of the Order is extremely attractive and feminine in appearance, consisting of an oval surround of pearls and in the centre the cypher VRI set in diamonds, pearls and turquoises. The Order was always returnable to the Crown on death, but it seems likely that those in possession of the insignia after the Second World War might have been allowed to retain them.

10 CROWN OF INDIA

11 ROYAL VICTORIAN ORDER
(a) (*below*) Star, 1st
class

11 (b) (*right*) Sash
badge

11 **The Royal Victorian Order** This was the last of the Orders instituted during the 19th century, and the award was the sole prerogative of the sovereign. It was found necessary to introduce such an award owing to the increasing influence exercised by Prime Ministers over the remaining Orders. The Victorian Order was introduced for award to British and Foreign subjects alike (who were admitted as honorary members), without embracing any political motives.

The Order consists of five classes, plus three different classes of medals of the Order which are available to both ladies and gentlemen.

In addition, there is a very special and rare distinction known as The Royal Victorian Chain. This was introduced a little later, in 1902, by Edward VII, and was given to selected foreign Princes and very high-ranking members of the Royal household.

12 **The Order of the British Empire** is the junior of all the British Orders being founded as recently as 1917. The Order was introduced owing to the large demand for honours and awards in this country and the commonwealth caused by the First World War. In many ways the problem was the same as that faced by the Prince Regent in 1814, following the Napoleonic Wars, when the Order of the Bath was enlarged.

Today the Order and its medals are awarded for services to the state and commonwealth generally. They are also given to a large number of people for valuable work in the social services and local government work.

As those to be rewarded were both service personnel and civilians, military and civil divisions were formed, the military being distinguished by an extra narrow stripe of pearl grey in the centre. Originally, the insignia contained Britannia in the centre, but in 1937 it was altered to incorporate the crowned effigies of Queen Mary and King George V. At the same time the

12 BRITISH EMPIRE
(a) Star, 2nd class, 1st type

12 (b) Neck badge, 2nd type

original purple riband was changed to the present-day
rose pink with pearl grey edges. As with the Victorian
Order, medals of the Order were introduced and were
awarded for gallantry or meritorious service.

The Order of the Companion of Honour might **13**
be described as something in the nature of a junior
Order of Merit. Founded by King George V in 1917
at the same time as the Order of the British Empire, it is
restricted to 65 members, both men and women, who
perform special service of national importance.

13 COMPANION OF HONOUR

14 NOVA SCOTIA BARONET'S BADGE

Appointments are made on the recommendations of the Prime Ministers of the countries of the British Commonwealth in accordance with the following statutory quotas: U.K. 45, Australia 7, New Zealand 2, other Commonwealth countries 11. The oval silver gilt and enamel badge is worn around the neck, the design incorporating an oak tree with the royal arms and, on the left, a knight in armour mounted on a horse. The surrounding blue enamel border bears the motto 'IN ACTION FAITHFUL AND IN HONOUR CLEAR'. The statutes ordain that the badge is to be worn on all occasions when decorations are worn, but it was not anticipated that any member would *also* be a holder of the Order of Merit which, too, is worn around the neck, on such occasions. In over half a century only two persons have been in receipt of both—Lord Attlee and Sir Winston Churchill.

Baronets' Badges The first badge introduced was
by the Baronets of Scotland who were known as
Baronets of Nova Scotia owing to the grant of lands
made to them by James I in 1624. It was not until
almost 300 years later that King George V granted
permission for Baronets of England, of Ireland, of
Great Britain and of the United Kingdom to wear a
distinctive badge to indicate their rank.

All the neck badges are oval in shape. In the Scottish
badge, worn from a tawny riband, the motto surrounds
a crowned shield carrying the cross of St Andrew.

The remaining badges, authorized in 1929, contain on
a central shield the crowned arms of Ulster surrounded
by a border of roses (England), or shamrocks (Ireland),
or roses and thistles combined (Great Britain), or roses,
thistles and shamrocks combined (United Kingdom).
All are worn from an orange riband with narrow dark
blue edges.

Knight Bachelor's Badges The Imperial Society of
Knight Bachelor's obtained, in 1926, the permission of

15 KNIGHT BACHELOR'S
BADGE
Neck badge (1974)

King George V to wear a distinctive badge so as to distinguish their rank, thus bringing them into line with the Baronets.

The badge is oval in shape and is worn on the left breast by means of a brooch pin on the reverse. Originally the badge was larger than the current model, measuring 3 inches by 2 inches in width. The centre contains a sheathed sword and belt plus spurs, on a red enamel background, the whole contained within an oval scroll surround. The title 'Knight Bachelor' was introduced by Henry III to signify that the title dies with the holder.

As the badge has always been worn on the left breast, recipients have always felt at a slight disadvantage to the wearers of neck badges. Consequently, in 1973, Queen Elizabeth II gave approval for the badges to be worn around the neck from a bright red riband edged with pale yellow. In addition, miniatures of the badge are now allowed.

16 **The Royal Family Orders** are, as the title infers, restricted solely to members (female) of the Royal Family. They were introduced by King George IV. All are individually made and therefore vary to a certain extent in execution and appearance. The distinguishing feature of the badges is the fine hand-painted portrait of the sovereign which is contained in a setting of diamonds. The badges are all worn on the left breast, suspended from a riband in the form of a bow. The older female members of the Royal Family may, of course, be entitled to wear badges awarded by more than one sovereign.

17 **The Royal Order of Victoria and Albert** was founded in 1862 and awarded by the Queen and her husband, the Prince Consort. The order embraced four classes which were awarded according to the social rank of the recipient as well as the services performed. The common feature of these very rare badges was the

16 GEORGE VI Decoration worn by H.M. the Queen

17 VICTORIA & ALBERT
2nd class badge

central conjoint effigies of Victoria and Albert, combined with a surround or part surround of precious stones. The fourth class, however, was much simpler as it contained the monogram 'V' and 'A', with small pearls.

18 **The Order of St John of Jerusalem** The Order was incorporated in the United Kingdom by Queen Victoria under a Royal Charter of 1888, the insignia being awarded by the Order and not the sovereign or the Crown, although the Queen is the Sovereign Head or Patron of the Order. Consequently the Order can be regarded as a semi-private Order.

The insignia is awarded for voluntary work in connection with the Priory's activities in hospital, ambulance and relief work. Persons who are not British subjects or who are non-Christians are made associates of the Order, the insignia being distinguished by a central white stripe on the otherwise plain black riband.

18 ST JOHN OF JERUSALEM
Serving Brother's badge

DECORATIONS FOR GALLANTRY
AND MERITORIOUS SERVICE

Victoria Cross   The foremost British and Common- **19**
wealth gallantry decoration is awarded for very exceptional gallantry and, as such, is the most prized
award that any subject can earn.

Prior to the Crimean War there was no recognized
gallantry medal, but the individual deeds of heroism in
this war made such an award necessary.   Consequently,
the Victoria Cross was instituted by Royal Warrant
dated 29 January 1856, and was made available to officers
and men alike.   It was deemed by Queen Victoria that
the cross should be simple in design and was to be made

19   VICTORIA CROSS

from the bronze cannon captured during the Crimean War. Victoria's interest in the award was such that she personally invested 62 of the 111 Crimean recipients at a parade held in Hyde Park. At one time Naval recipients wore their award suspended from a Navy blue riband and the Army from a crimson riband, the latter being identical to the Army long service medal. It was only in 1916 that a miniature of the cross was added to the riband in undress uniform so as to make it more distinctive, and in 1918 the crimson riband was adopted by all Services.

The award is open to civilians (four were awarded during the Indian Mutiny) and also to women, but no award has ever been made. The cross has been earned on three occasions in the U.K., and a small number have been won by men of foreign origin. Three cases of both father and son receiving the award are recorded and four known cases of brothers. Perhaps the most outstanding are the three recipients who were awarded the V.C. with bar. To date 1,349 Crosses and three bars have been awarded.

20 New Zealand Cross This decoration for gallantry is unique to the Commonwealth of New Zealand, being awarded on 23 occasions only for bravery during the period of the Second Maori Wars from 1860–72, although the last award was not approved until 1910. The story of the introduction and phasing out of this award is an interesting one. A recommendation for the V.C. was forwarded to London by the Officer commanding the Forces in New Zealand, Lt.-Col. Sir Henry Havelock, who himself had won the V.C. The recommendation of Capt. Charles Heaphy of the Auckland Militia was refused on the grounds that he was not of the regular forces of the Crown. However, by Royal Warrant of 1 January 1867 the V.C. was then extended to members of local forces when serving with Imperial troops *and* under the command of a general or

20 NEW ZEALAND CROSS
(a) (*left*) obverse

20 (b) (*right*) reverse

other officer (of the Crown). As a result Capt. Heaphy's V.C. was then allowed, this being the first to a member of a colonial force as well as being the first to a non-regular service man. British forces and officers were then withdrawn before the conclusion of the Maori wars, and although further acts of gallantry were performed by local forces, V.C.s could not be awarded as the local forces were not serving with Imperial forces and were not under the command of a regular officer of the Crown.

Consequently Col. Whitmore, Commandant of the New Zealand Armed Constabulary, suggested the purchase of a limited number of rosettes and chevrons for the Constabulary. From this most modest suggestion, the New Zealand Cross was developed and instituted by an Order in Council made at Government House, Wellington, on 10 March 1869, the intention being that it was to be recognized as a purely local 'unofficial' award, such as the Royal Geographical and Humane Societies awards, and was not to be compared with those honours issued by the Crown.

Awards were made immediately, and before the approval of London could be obtained. The Secretary of State's (Earl Granville) reaction was prompt and took place in the form of a dispatch to the Governor, extracts of which read 'I am unwillingly constrained to observe that in complying with this natural desire (to reward local forces) you have overstepped the limits of the authority confided to you by Her Majesty'.

'The authority inherent in the Queen as the fountain head of honour throughout her Empire has never been delegated to you, and you are therefore not competent, as Her Majesty's representative, to create any of those titular or decorative distinctions which, in the British Empire, have their source, and are valuable because they have their source, in the grace of the Sovereign.' After these and similar remarks, which established who was the fountain head, the Secretary of State then went on to say that the Queen gave her blessing to the New Zealand Cross. By 1911 the forces upon whose members the Cross could be conferred, such as the Armed Constabulary, Militia and Volunteers had all been disbanded and, consequently, the Cross which is the rarest of Commonwealth gallantry awards, fell naturally into disuse.

21 The George Cross

Instituted in 1940 to replace the rare and almost unknown Empire Gallantry medal. The demands made on the civilian population from the summer of 1940 made it necessary to acknowledge extreme and outstanding gallantry. All our other awards were for gallantry in the face of the enemy, with the exception of the A.F.C. and A.F.M. awarded for service in the air, and also the Albert medals given solely for saving life. King George VI wished to introduce a civilian award which would have the same respect as the V.C. without adding to the number of awards already in existence.

21 GEORGE CROSS

The outcome of the various suggestions was the George Cross, which was to be next in seniority to the Victoria Cross, and which was to replace the E.G.M. Recipients of this latter award exchanged their medals for the G.C. Consequently some of the 'replacement' G.C.s won their awards some eighteen years before the G.C. was introduced. In more recent years the G.C. has superseded both types and classes of the Albert medal, recipients of these medals exchanging them for the G.C.

The award has been very sparingly given like its service counterpart, the V.C., fewer than 140 having been given to date in a period of over 30 years, including the war years of 1940–5, but excluding the exchange awards. Some of the most well-known G.C. recipients are Wing Cmdr. Yeo-Thomas, Violette Szabo and Odette Sansom for their incredible exploits in enemy-occupied territory. The Earl of Suffolk and Berkshire's exploits with unexploded bombs are another case where a G.C. 'story' would fill a book.

22 Distinguished Service Order After the campaigns of the mid-19th century such as the Crimea and the Indian Mutiny, it was realized that no adequate award for distinguished services was available to junior officers apart from the V.C. and, in the case of Majors and above, the C.B. Consequently, the Distinguished Service Order was instituted in 1886. Since that date the basic design has remained the same apart from the obverse central crown and the reverse royal cypher which has changed with each sovereign. It was originally issued in gold and enamel, but some two or three years afterwards the award was issued, in common with other British awards, in silver-gilt and enamel. Naturally, awards in gold are rare, as indeed are those awarded during the reign of Edward VII, owing to the fact that no major wars took place.

In common with some other service awards the D.S.O. is not awarded to civilians, although officers of the Merchant Navy can qualify during time of war.

To distinguish those who have gained additional awards, a bar is attached to the riband of the award. The maximum number of bars to one cross is three thus representing four D.S.O.s; only eight have ever been awarded.

22 DISTINGUISHED SERVICE
ORDER
obverse

23 ROYAL RED CROSS
Associates (2nd class) badge

23 **Royal Red Cross** Approved by Queen Victoria in 1883 as a distinction for award to British or foreign ladies for exceptional service in the field of Naval and Military nursing. Originally the award was in gold and enamel, but after about 1887 it was made in silver gilt and enamel. The red enamel cross contains on the four arms 'FAITH', 'HOPE', 'CHARITY' and '1883', with the sovereign's effigy in the obverse centre and a cypher in the reverse centre. The award was recognized by the initials R.R.C.

During the period 1914–18, the need to award the Decoration to a vastly enlarged nursing service made it necessary to introduce a second class which was in silver and enamel, the recipients being known as 'Associates', or A.R.R.C.

24 **Distinguished Service Cross** Originally known as the Conspicuous Service Cross, it was instituted in 1901 as a result of proposals submitted by the Lords Commissioners of the Admiralty to King Edward VII. It was the opinion of the Admiralty that an award for issue to junior officers should be instituted as the D.S.O. would not normally be available to them. In 1914 the name of the decoration was altered to the D.S.C. In 1916 a bar to the cross was instituted, and in 1931 the award was extended to the Merchant Navy and Fishing Fleets. During the Second World War the cross was available to R.A.F. officers serving with the Fleet, and to Army officers who served the defensive anti-aircraft and submarine guns aboard Merchant vessels.

Like other gallantry awards to officers, the award carried no wording or naming. It was a simple frosted cross with a crowned royal cypher in the centre, the reverse being plain apart from hallmarks; those awarded after 1940 had the year of award engraved on them.

Only eight of the original C.S.C.s were awarded up to 1914. Approximately 2,000 D.S.C. awards were issued for 1914–18, and about 5,000 for the period

24 DISTINGUISHED SERVICE
CROSS
(a) (*right*) George VI
issue with 2nd award bar

24 (b) (*left*) Elizabeth II
issue

1939–45, which reflects the more arduous part played by the Navy in the Second World War.

The Military Cross The Army, unlike the Royal 25 Navy who possessed the D.S.C., did not have a gallantry award for issue to junior commissioned officers or warrant officers at the beginning of the 1914–18 war. The demands for such an award caused by the First World War made it necessary to institute the Military Cross by Royal Warrant dated 28 December 1914.

The M.C., like the D.S.C., is very simple in design being a cross of silver having on each arm the Imperial Crown and in the centre the sovereign's cypher. The riband is distinctive, being three equal stripes of white, purple, white. The award is available to all Commonwealth and Colonial forces, which use the same design. In common with the other awards reserved for one branch of the services, the M.C. has been awarded to the R.N. and members of the R.A.F. for services on the ground. During the period of the First World War over 40,000 crosses were awarded, including four with three bars. In the period 1939–45 approximately 11,000 were issued.

25 MILITARY CROSS
(a) (*left*) George V issue

25 (b) (*right*) George VI issue

The Distinguished Flying Cross Following the **26**
formation of the Royal Air Force on 1 April 1918, the
D.F.C. was introduced in June of the same year to
recognize gallantry whilst flying in active operations
against the enemy. Prior to this date officers were
awarded the M.C. When originally introduced the
ribbon was composed of blue and white horizontal
stripes, but this was altered in July 1919 to diagonal
stripes running at an angle of 45 degrees. In 1941 the
award was extended to Fleet Air Arm air crew serving
with the R.A.F. and from February 1942 onwards it
could be given to personnel of Dominion countries.

The award is in the form of an ornate silver cross, the
horizontal arms representing the wings of a bird and the
vertical arms an aircraft propeller; the cypher of the
reigning monarch is contained in the reverse centre.
From 1918 to 1939 just over 1,200 awards were made
and during the period 1939-45 approximately 22,000,

which of course reflects the greatly enlarged force and six years of very extensive activity. The award was occasionally given to the Navy and the Army, including a number to the glider pilots for their services during the Second World War at Arnhem and elsewhere. Naturally these crosses, and those awarded for such actions as the Battle of Britain, or for a specific act, are more sought after than those sometimes awarded at the end of a tour or tours of active flying duty.

27 Air Force Cross This award was instituted in June 1918 at the same time as the D.F.C., D.F.M. and A.F.M. Thus four gallantry awards altogether were available to the R.A.F. The A.F.C.s role was to reward those who distinguished themselves in the air though not in active operations against the enemy. The Air Force was an exception in that constant risk to life was undertaken not only in experimental work, but in day to day

27 AIR FORCE CROSS
George V issue

training, navigational and flying exercises.

As with the other three awards, the first riband was comprised of horizontal red and white stripes, which were shortly afterwards superseded by diagonal stripes. The silver cross is unusually large for a 'medal', consisting of a thunderbolt in the form of a cross, the arms conjoined by wings, the base bar terminating with a bomb surmounted by another cross composed of aeroplane propellers; the four ends contain the cypher of the reigning monarch. The cross in common with the D.F.C. was issued unnamed.

From the date of institution until 1939 just over 850 were awarded, including 12 first bars and 3 with second bars. From 1940–5 just over 2,000 were awarded, and since 1945 just over 2,000. Two interesting awards were to F/Lt. M. J. Adam for a new altitude record of 53,937 feet in 1938, and to the Duke of Hamilton for being the first to fly over Mount Everest in 1934.

28 ORDER OF BRITISH
INDIA
1st class

28 **The Order of British India** This award was introduced by the Honourable East India Company in 1837 to reward its Indian officers for outstanding long and meritorious service. It consisted of two classes, both of them in gold and enamel which were worn around the neck from a crimson ribbon that was originally sky-blue. However, a light blue ribbon was not found to be practical owing to the habit among all classes of natives of oiling the hair, which soiled the ribbon. After the partition of India and Pakistan in 1946, it is curious to note that the Pakistan Government ordered a quantity, from the London medallists Spink & Son Ltd., for award to British officers who had rendered outstanding services. Thus the donors and recipients of the award were completely reversed.

29 **Kaiser-i-Hind** Introduced in 1900 by Queen Victoria for award to those, irrespective of nationality,

29 KAISER-I-HIND
Edward VII issue

30 ALBERT MEDAL
Saving Life at sea issue,
2nd class

colour, creed or sex, who had performed useful public service in India, this being frequently issued for social work and similar services. The decoration in gold, was awarded by the Sovereign on the recommendation of the Secretary of State for India, and in silver, was awarded by the Governor-General. Upon the partition of India, in 1947, the award was abolished.

The oval award contains the cypher of the reigning Monarch surmounted by a crown; the reverse contains 'KAISER-I-HIND' and 'FOR PUBLIC SERVICE IN INDIA'. The award was worn from riband fashioned into a bow when awarded to a lady.

Albert Medal Named after Prince Albert, the Prince **30** Consort, who died in 1861. Four different types were given, although when it was originally instituted in 1866 it was awarded for gallantry in saving life at sea, 1st and 2nd class, and then extended in 1867 to cover actions on land. The general esteem that this award was held in, earned it the unofficial name of the 'civilian V.C.'

Like the V.C., the decoration entitled one to a gratuity, irrespective of class. In 1968 this was £100.

The 1st class was abolished in 1949 in favour of the G.C., and more recently all those entitled to the 2nd class have had the decoration changed for the G.C.

The youngest recipients were Anthony Fraser, aged eight, and Dorothy Ashburnum, aged 11, who saved each other's lives when attacked by a cougar in Canada; and David Western, aged 10, who attempted to save the lives of three companions who had fallen through the ice of a frozen lake.

The following summary of awards will illustrate the past difficulty of earning this decoration.

Gold	Sea	24	*Silver*	Sea	209
	Land	45		Land	282

31 The King's (and Queen's) Medal for Bravery (South Africa) This was introduced as recently as 1939, to reward acts of life-saving within South Africa, or in territories administered by the Union. Two classes were introduced, the first being in gold and the second in silver. The obverse carried the effigy and title of the sovereign, and the reverse a design depicting the rescue, on horseback, by Wolraad Woltemade in the year 1773, of persons in danger of drowning in Table Bay; the words 'FOR BRAVERY', in English, and 'VIR DAPPERHEID' in Afrikaans, also appear. The medal, which was abolished upon South Africa becoming a Republic, has only been awarded once in gold and on 35 occasions in silver.

32 Distinguished Conduct Medal It was the Crimean War which caused this award, for other ranks only, to be instituted in December 1854. Prior to this date no medal was available to reward individual acts of gallan-

31 KING'S (AND QUEEN'S) MEDAL FOR BRAVERY, SOUTH AFRICA
reverse

32 DISTINGUISHED CONDUCT MEDAL
reverse

try in the Army. The D.C.M. has been awarded to civilians but never to women. Before 1894 the D.C.M. was available to Dominion and Colonial Forces, but after this date each country awarded its own, which contained distinctive titles on the reverse.

The numbers given for the various campaigns since the award was instituted vary considerably. For instance, some 770 were issued for the Crimean War, but fewer than 10 for the whole of the Indian Mutiny period. 2,892 were awarded during the reign of Victoria including 2,050 for the Boer War, of which a number were issued with the effigy of Edward VII on them. As a comparison, approximately 25,000 were awarded for the First World War and fewer than 1,900 for the Second. Additional awards are represented by a bar attached to the riband. Only 10 medals were awarded with 2 bars, representing 3 awards to each.

33 Conspicuous Gallantry Medal (Naval and Air Force)

The Naval award had two separate phases. The first was the introduction of the award for operations in the Baltic and the Crimea, for the war against Russia 1854–6. However, following the introduction of the Victoria Cross in 1856, no further awards of the C.G.M. were made and it fell into disuse until it was re-instituted in 1874. Only 11 of the original awards were made to 10 recipients (one received it twice). The Meritorious Service Medal was used, the wording 'MERITORIOUS SERVICE' on the reverse being erased and 'CONSPICUOUS GALLANTRY' engraved, the first die-struck word 'FOR' remained. Following the successful conclusion of the Ashantee War, 1873–4, the award was resurrected, a special die being cut for the reverse with the words 'FOR CONSPICUOUS GALLANTRY' in relief. Since 1874 the medal has been awarded very sparingly, only 234 having been given, including 108 for the period 1914–19 and 72 for 1940–6.

During the Second World War it was realized that

the D.F.M. was not sufficient to cover the deeds performed by N.C.O.s and men, consequently the C.G.M. was extended to the R.A.F. It is the same as the naval medal in all respects except that it is worn from a light blue ribbon with dark blue edges, as opposed to the naval white riband with dark blue edges. From 1943–5 only 103 awards were made, which was very few in view of the vastly enlarged R.A.F. at this time. Since 1946 it is believed that only one award has been authorized.

The George Medal Instituted 24 September 1940 (the same day as the George Cross). At that time there was a particular need to reward a great many heroes in all walks of life. However, it was the intention of the authorities that the G.C. should stand supreme and that its position as the 'civilian V.C.' should not be undermined by the award of large numbers. The result

34

33 CONSPICUOUS GALLANTRY MEDAL reverse

was that the George Medal was introduced as a 'junior' to the G.C., its position of seniority being after the Conspicuous Gallantry Medal. The medal was awarded for lesser acts of gallantry which did not warrant the award of the George Cross. The award is in the shape of a circular silver medal. The obverse depicts the effigy of the sovereign, whilst the reverse shows St George slaying the dragon on the coast of England. The riband is red with five narrow stripes, the blue being 'borrowed' from the George Cross.

34 GEORGE MEDAL
reverse

35 The King's Police Medal

35 The Queen's Police and Fire Brigade Services Medal

35 The King's (Queen's) Police Medal
Until the year 1909 there was no award to recognize gallantry and distinguished service in the Police and

Fire Brigades, either in the United Kingdom or in the Empire. As a result, the King's Police Medal was introduced in 1909 by Edward VII to reward both heroic acts of courage and instances of conspicuous devotion to duty. However, in 1933 two distinct divisions were introduced namely 'FOR GALLANTRY' and 'FOR DISTINGUISHED SERVICE', the reverses of the medals containing this wording. At the same time red stripes were introduced to the ribbon to distinguish the gallantry recipients.

35 KING'S (AND QUEEN'S) POLICE MEDAL reverse, post-1933 issue For Gallantry

As with the Albert and Edward medals, it was later decided that the medal for gallantry should only be awarded posthumously. In 1954 separate medals were introduced for the Police and the Fire Brigades.

South Africa's King's Police Medal Introduced **36** in 1937 for gallantry and distinguished service in South Africa and South West Africa. The design was similar to the United Kingdom issue but the reverse wording was bilingual. From 1937–60, 30 gallantry and 17 distinguished service medals were awarded.

36 SOUTH AFRICA KING'S POLICE MEDAL reverse

37 Queen's Fire Service Medal Instituted by Royal Warrant dated 19 May 1954. As with the Queen's Police Medal, two different issues were introduced namely 'FOR GALLANTRY' and 'FOR DISTINGUISHED FIRE SERVICE'. Fewer than 300 distinguished service medals have been awarded and, it is believed that there have been no awards for gallantry.

38 The Edward Medal Originally introduced in 1907 to reward acts of gallantry in mines and quarries, and extended in 1909 to include industry generally. Both medals were awarded in silver and bronze; all contained the effigy of the reigning monarch on the obverse. The miners issue contained on the reverse a design representing the rescue of a miner and the inscription 'FOR

38 EDWARD MEDAL
(a) reverse, second type, industrial issue

38 (b) reverse, miners issue

COURAGE'. The Industrial issue included a classical female figure holding a wreath, with the words 'FOR COURAGE' and a suggestion of a manufacturing town in low relief in the background.

In 1940, owing to the institution of the George Cross and George Medal, awards for civilian acts became confusing. Consequently, in 1949, King George VI decreed that the silver medal should cease and that all future bronze medals would be awarded posthumously.

The rarest award is the silver Industrial issue. Only 25 have been awarded as opposed to 77 for miners. The total of silver and bronze medals issued, of both types, was 583.

39 **Indian Distinguished Service Medal** Introduced in 1907 as an award to recognize distinguished services of Indian commissioned and non-commissioned officers, and also men of the regular land forces of India.

39 INDIAN DISTINGUISHED SERVICE MEDAL reverse

40 DISTINGUISHED
SERVICE MEDAL
(a) (*left*)
obverse,
George V

40 (b) (*right*)
reverse

In 1929 the award was extended to the Royal Indian Marines, and in 1940 to the Indian Air Force. Furthermore it was again extended in 1944 to include the Hong Kong and Singapore Royal Artillery.

The silver medal contains the crowned effigy of the sovereign and, on the reverse, 'FOR DISTINGUISHED SERVICE' within a wreath. Just over 5,300 awards were made including some 50 bars from 1907 until the medal was cancelled following the independence of India and Pakistan, in 1947.

The Distinguished Service Medal   This is a further   **40**

gallantry award introduced as a result of the heavy demands made by the First World War. The D.S.M. was introduced for award to the naval ratings and Royal Marines who distinguished themselves in time of war. It was intended that this should be junior to the rare Conspicuous Gallantry medal. In 1916 a second award bar was introduced, and in 1940 N.C.O.s and men of the R.A.F. were made eligible. It was later extended to the Army serving afloat and to the Merchant Marine.

During the First World War approximately 5,600 were awarded, including two with two second award bars. In the period 1939–45 just under 7,300 were issued, including one with three bars. Those awarded for such actions as Jutland, the Falkland Islands and Zeebrugge during the 1914–18 War, the destruction of the Scharnhorst, the naval landings and submarine actions of 1939–45, as well as Yangtze, 1949, etc., are some of the actions for which D.S.M.s were awarded, and which are particularly attractive to collectors.

41 MILITARY MEDAL
reverse, George VI issue

Military Medal Instituted in March 1916 for award to N.C.O.s and men for individual or associated acts of bravery in the field; in June of the same year it was extended to women. Being junior to the D.C.M. rather more have been issued, it being recognized that this is the most common of the British gallantry awards. Over 120,000 were awarded in the period 1914–18, which probably signifies the appalling close combat battles lasting for four years. Just under 16,000 were issued for 1939–45.

As with all other gallantry awards, many have been awarded for post 1939–45 operations in places such as Palestine, Malaya, Aden, Brunei, Korea and Northern Ireland. The medal is attractive, being silver with a scroll-like suspender worn from a blue riband with three central white and two red stripes. The effigy of the reigning monarch appears on the obverse, while the reverse carries 'FOR BRAVERY IN THE FIELD', with the crowned royal cypher above, all within a wreath.

The Distinguished Flying Medal was introduced at the same time, and for the same reasons as the D.F.C., the medal being available to air crew N.C.O.s and men for acts of valour, courage or devotion to duty whilst flying in active operations against the enemy.

The silver medal is oval in shape, the obverse carrying the effigy and title of the sovereign, while the reverse depicts a representation of the goddess Athena Nike seated on an aeroplane. The riband is identical to the officers' D.F.C., but the diagonal stripes are narrower. Unlike the D.F.C., the Distinguished Flying Medal has always been issued named, having the service number, rank, initials, surname and service, the latter indicating the Commonwealth.

As a large majority of air crew have always been commissioned officers, the number of D.F.M.s awarded has been fewer than the D.F.C. Fewer than 200 were

42 DISTINGUISHED
FLYING MEDAL
reverse

issued prior to 1939, and from then until 1945 there were approximately 6,700.

43 **The Air Force Medal** This is the junior of the four purely Royal Air Force Awards being issued to N.C.O.s and men in exactly the same way and for the same reasons as the Air Force Cross. The rather large oval medal is struck in silver; the obverse contains the bust and legend of the reigning sovereign. The reverse depicts Hermes mounted on a hawk, which is in flight; the surround consists of a wreath of laurel. Like the D.F.M. but unlike the D.F.C. and A.F.C., this medal is issued with the service numbers, rank, surname and initials engraved around the edge. As even fewer N.C.O.s and men were in a position to earn the A.F.C., this has been awarded on fewer occasions in all than the D.F.M. Only 204 were awarded up to 1939, including five bars, and from 1939 to date approximately 630. A typical example of the coverage of this award is the 10 awarded for outstanding services and heroism during the Berlin airlift of 1948.

Indian Order of Merit   This is the oldest gallantry **44** award, and it was introduced as far back as 1837 by the Honourable East India Company.   However, it did not become an official award until the H.E.I. Company's forces were taken over by the Crown, after the conclusion of the Indian Mutiny.   At this time the Order of British India was established (this 'honourable service' award is dealt with in item 28).

Three classes were originally introduced, the first in gold, the second and third in silver, all with the obverse centres enamelled.

In 1902 a Civil division was introduced, but the award was reduced to one class only in 1939, as was the Military division in 1944.   The award was first known as

43   AIR FORCE MEDAL obverse, Elizabeth II

the Order of Merit, but this was altered in 1902 to the Indian Order of Merit to distinguish it from the (Imperial) Order of Merit.

In 1911 the Victoria Cross was made available to the Indian forces and as a result the first class of the I.O.M. was abolished.

44 INDIAN ORDER OF MERIT obverse

45 Burma Gallantry Medal This award was introduced in 1940, and owing to the granting of independence to Burma, the last awards were announced in 1947. During its lifetime just over 200 awards were given including three second award bars.

The award was conferred by The Governor of Burma upon the officers, non-commissioned officers and other ranks of the Burma Army, the Frontier Force, the Military Police, the Burma Royal Naval Volunteer Reserve and the Auxiliary Air Force for an act of

45 (*left*) BURMA GALLANTRY
MEDAL
reverse

46 (*right*) SEA GALLANTRY
MEDAL
reverse

conspicuous gallantry performed in connection with
their duties.

The silver medal was 1·4 inches in diameter and bore
an effigy of King George VI and legend on the obverse,
and 'BURMA FOR GALLANTRY' with a laurel wreath on
the reverse. The medal was suspended from a scroll-
like bar and a dark green riband with a central crimson
stripe.

Sea Gallantry Medal Originally introduced by the **46**
Board of Trade in 1854 and is the only gallantry medal

instituted by Act of Parliament. The silver and bronze medals were $2\frac{1}{4}$ inches in diameter without ribbon, but after King Edward VII began to take a personal interest in the award and to present some of them himself, the size was reduced to $1\frac{1}{4}$ inches, which is less than the present-day standard size; at the same time they were to be worn from a ribbon.

47 Burma Police Medal Burma was made independent from India in 1937 when it became a separate colony. It was then found necessary to introduce a gallantry award which was given to the fire brigades, in addition to the police force. The maximum number that could be awarded in any one year was 25.

The standard size bronze medal bore the effigy of King George VI with a legend on the obverse, and on the reverse 'BURMA POLICE FOR DISTINGUISHED CONDUCT' within a crowned wreath, in a very similar pattern to its Indian counterpart. From 1937 until the granting of independence to Burma approximately 140 awards were made.

48 Indian Police Medal Instituted in 1932 to reward the Indian Police Forces and Fire Brigades for services of conspicuous merit. The King's Police Medal was available, but it was found to be too restrictive as only 50 awards could be made each year for the Indian Forces. After 1944 two different types of medal were isued: (a) 'FOR GALLANTRY' and (b) 'FOR MERITORIOUS SERVICE'. Prior to this date one common reverse was used with 'FOR DISTINGUISHED CONDUCT' on the reverse. The medals were awarded after the creation of the Dominion of India in 1947, but ceased when India became a Republic in 1950.

49 Colonial Police Medal Introduced in 1938 to recognize acts of distinguished conduct in the Police and Fire Brigades in the Colonies and Territories administered by the United Kingdom. The silver medal contained

47 (*right*)   BURMA POLICE
MEDAL
reverse

48 (*below*)   INDIAN POLICE
MEDAL
pre-1944 reverse

49 (*right*)   COLONIAL POLICE
MEDAL
reverse

the usual sovereign's effigy and legend on the obverse, while the reverse contained either (a) a police truncheon and wreath surrounded by 'COLONIAL POLICE FORCES FOR GALLANTRY', or (b) a fireman's helmet, axe and wreath with 'COLONIAL FIRE BRIGADES. FOR GALLANTRY' surrounding. The ribands are the same as the Colonial M.S.M., but have an additional red stripe in the centre. Medals awarded to the Fire Brigade are considerably rarer than those to the Police, the ratio being about 1 to 38.

51 MEDAL OF THE ORDER OF THE BRITISH EMPIRE
Meritorious Service issue (No. 51), civil division riband

50 **Medal of the Order of the British Empire for Gallantry** Normally known as the Empire Gallantry medal, which was introduced in 1922. Prior to 1940, when the Gallantry medal was superseded by the George Cross, it was awarded on 130 occasions only. The award, like the Order of Knighthood itself, had

two separate divisions: Military and Civil. The former was distinguished by a narrow central red stripe and, after July 1937, by an extra pearl grey central stripe. In 1937 the riband was changed from purple to pink with pearl grey edges, the Military division having an extra stripe in the centre.

Medal of the Order of the British Empire for Meritorious Service 51

introduced at the same time as the Gallantry award mentioned above. The only difference was on the reverse where the word 'GALLANTRY' was replaced by 'MERITORIOUS SERVICE'. However, unlike the Gallantry medal which was superseded by the G.C., this award for Meritorious Service is still given.

ADDENDUM

Queen's Gallantry Medal

Introduced in 1974 for award to all British and Commonwealth servicemen and civilians. The primary intention is to make the decoration available for actions for which purely military honours are not normally granted.

The award is made available to civilians on the recommendation of the Prime Minister and the First Lord of the Treasury, and for members of the Armed Forces via the Secretary of State for Defence, or by the appropriate Minister of State for Commonwealth countries.

The intention is to award the medal for exceptional acts of bravery. The medal itself is circular in form and in silver. The obverse carries the crowned effigy of the Sovereign, and the reverse a design of laurel leaves and the words 'The Queen's Gallantry Medal', which is surmounted by a crown. The riband is $1\frac{1}{4}''$ in width, of dark blue with a central stripe of pearl grey, the pearl grey stripe containing in its centre a narrow stripe of rose pink. The award entitles recipients to place the initials Q.G.M. after their names.

CAMPAIGN MEDALS

————◆◆◆————

Honourable East India Company's Medals, 1778–1837   This remarkable Company, born in 1599 by an association of merchant adventurers in London, for the purpose of trading with the Far East, later assumed the power and proportions of imperial magnificence.   The gigantic power that it wielded until just after the Indian Mutiny (1856–7) made it necessary for it to maintain a large and efficient army and navy to not only guard its immediate local possessions and factories, but to ensure their continued safety by enlarging their territories until they reached a stage where they controlled most of the Indian sub-continent.   This in turn brought the Company into conflict with neighbouring countries as well as having to contest territories claimed by the French and other nations.

It is to this Company that we are indebted for the example it set of issuing campaign or service medals long before the first British Government's general issue alike to officers and men, namely that for Waterloo 1815.   The medals, except that for Burma 1824–6, were often of two sizes with simple ring suspenders and without standard ribands as we know them today. Consequently the earlier medals have been listed separately, the later standard size medals with conventional suspenders, bars, clasps and ribands being contained in the later section of British Government issues.

★   ★   ★

52 **Deccan, 1778–84**   The obverse depicts Britannia seated and holding a wreath, the design also including a fort which is flying the Union Flag.   The reverse

52 DECCAN 1778–84
obverse

contains a Persian inscription reading:

'The courage and exertions of those valiant men by whom the name of Englishmen has been celebrated and exalted from Hindostan to the Deccan having been established throughout the world, this has been granted by the Government of Calcutta, in commemoration of the excellent services of the brave; year of the Hegira, 1199, A.D. 1784.'

The silver medals were struck in Calcutta and were either 1·6 inches or 1·25 inches in diameter; the larger size, a few of which were in gold, were issued to officers only.

This was the first of the Company's general issue of medals, and it was awarded for service in Western India and Gujerat, under the overall leadership of Warren Hastings.

Mysore Campaign, 1790–2   Struck in two sizes, 1·7 **53** inches and 1·5 inches, in diameter. The larger was awarded in gold and silver; the smaller in silver only. The obverse depicts a Sepoy holding a Union Flag and the flag of Mysore with the fortress of Seringapatam in the background. The reverse contains a wreath of

FOR SERVICES ON THE ISLAND OF CEYLON A.D. 1795/6.

laurel and within, an inscription 'FOR SERVICES IN MYSORE A.D. 1791–2'. A Persian inscription surrounds the laurel wreath. The medal was awarded to the officers and men under Lord Cornwallis and Generals Meadows and Abercromby for the defeat of the powerful Tippoo Sahib, Ruler of Mysore.

54 Capture of Ceylon, 1795   Two medals were awarded in gold to Captains Barton and Clarke, and in silver to 121 native gunners of the Bengal Artillery for their services during the capture of the island of Ceylon from the Dutch. This campaign came about as a result of the Napoleonic Wars.

The 2-inch medal bore on the obverse an inscription

'FOR SERVICES ON THE ISLAND OF CEYLON A.D. 1795–6'
and there was a similar inscription, but in Persian, on
the reverse.

Seringapatam, 1799 Awarded to both British and **55**
Indian regiments for the capture of the fortress of
Seringapatam on the 4 May 1799. Tippoo Sahib,
Ruler of Mysore, who had been defeated in the campaign of 1790–2 was attacked as a result of his hostile
movements and negotiations with the French.   The left
wing in the attack was under the command of Lt.-Col.
the Honourable Arthur Wellesley, later the Duke of
Wellington, and it was one of the actions which later
gained him the nickname of 'The Sepoy General'.
As a result of the campaign the kingdom of Mysore was
added to the territory administered by the Honourable
East India Company.   One result of the capture of the

55 SERINGAPATAM 1799
obverse

fortress was the distribution of prize money which ranged from £100,000 for the Commander-in-Chief to £7 for private soldiers!

The medals were awarded in gold, silver gilt, silver, bronze and pewter. The obverse depicted a fight between the British lion and Tippoo Sahib's tiger, with the Roman date in the exergue. The reverse showed a fine scene of the attack on the fortress.

56 EGYPT 1801
(a) (*left*) obverse

56 (b) (*right*) reverse

56 Egypt, 1801 Sixteen gold and just over 2,000 silver medals, 1·9 inches in diameter, were awarded by the Company to the British and Indian Regiments under Major-General Sir David Baird.

At this time the French forces were dominating Egypt, which posed a threat to the freedom of India. The force from India, with supporting troops from the Cape of Good Hope, attacked Egypt from the south, while the forces from home under General Sir Ralph

Abercromby attacked from the Mediterranean.

The medals awarded by the Company bore on the obverse a sepoy holding a Union Flag with a Persian inscription in the exergue. The reverse depicted a ship in full sail, with the Pyramids, and in the exergue the date 'MDCCCI'.

57 RODRIGUES, ISLES OF BOURBON & FRANCE 1809–10 obverse

Capture of Rodrigues, Isle of Bourbon and Isle of France, 1809–10 57

Issued by the Company to its own regiments only in gold and silver, fewer than 50 of the former and just over 2,000 of the latter were awarded.

The medal, 1·9 inches in diameter, bears on the obverse a native holding a Union Flag while standing before a gun. The reverse contains a wreath, a Persian inscription and also one in English: 'RODRIGUES VI JULY MDCCCIX. BOURBON VII JULY AND ISLE OF FRANCE III DEC. MDCCCX'.

These medals were awarded for the capture of the three islands from the French by British troops and those of the Company from Bombay and Bengal, assisted by ships from the Royal Navy.

58 Java, 26 August 1811 This 2-inch medal was awarded in gold (133) and in silver (5,750) to the officers and
men of the Company's forces. The British forces were,
as late as 1848, issued with the Naval and Military
General Service medals with bar Java, the General and
Field Officers as well as Naval Captains having previously been awarded gold medals (Nos. 61 and 62).

The obverse of the Company's medal depicts a scene
of the attack on Fort Cornelis and the word 'CORNELIS'.
The reverse contains a Persian inscription and 'JAVA
CONQUERED XXVI AUGUST MDCCCXI'. The attack on
and capture of Java from Holland, which had at that
time become part of Napoleon's empire, was part of
the British Government's policy of dominating the
East at a time when European nations were largely contained in Europe by the Royal Navy's blockade.

59 Nepaul War Medal, 1814–16 This scarce 2-inch
medal was awarded in silver, and was issued to native
troops only. The obverse contains a scene of hills and
stockades, and the reverse a Persian inscription. The
British troops and also the native troops who did not
receive this medal were, in 1851, awarded the Army
of India medal with clasp Nepaul (No. 65).

The medal was granted for two campaigns in Nepaul
under Generals Marley, Wood, Gillespie (who was
killed) and Ochterlony. The campaign came about
because the Rajah of Nepaul had refused to ratify a
treaty which had been signed by his ambassadors; it was
also to combat the frequent border raids made on the
Company's territory. Since then, Gurkha troops from
Nepaul have been introduced into the Indian and British
armies and their outstanding bravery and loyalty has
become legendary.

60 Coorg Medal, 1837 This scarce medal, almost 2
inches in diameter, was awarded in gold and silver; only
44 of the former and 300 of the latter were issued.

The obverse depicts a Coorg holding a knife in his

58 JAVA 1811
obverse

59 (*above*) NEPAUL 1814–16
obverse

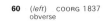

60 (*left*) COORG 1837
obverse

raised right hand and a musket in his left with an inscription in Canarese which translated reads 'A mark of favour given for loyalty to the Company's Government in suppressing rebellion in the months of April and May 1837'. The reverse contains war trophies and 'FOR DISTINGUISHED CONDUCT AND LOYALTY TO THE BRITISH GOVERNMENT, COORG APRIL 1837'.

The medal was restricted to the Coorgs who remained loyal during the rebellion, and was not awarded to the Company's regular or irregular forces.

* * *

61 **Naval Gold Medals** Introduced in 1795 some two years after the commencement of hostilities with France

61 NAVAL GOLD MEDAL
(a) (*below*) obverse

61 (b) (*above*) reverse

and 18 years before the equivalent Army gold crosses and medals. Officers so honoured and who were still living in 1848 also received the Naval General Service medal, but Army officers who qualified for the later Military Gold medals did not receive bars to the Military General Service medal in 1848.

These Naval Gold medals were first introduced for award to Admirals and Captains of Ships following Lord Howe's fleet victory over the French off Ushant on 1 June 1794, this being known as the 'Glorious First of June'. The larger medal, 2 inches in diameter, was awarded to Admirals, and the smaller, 1·3 inches, to Captains.

The medals are all rare and valuable as only 22 of the larger and 117 of the smaller were awarded. In addition, the Admirals present at Lord Howe's victory were awarded special gold chains with their medals. The medals were discontinued after 1815, the enlarged Order of the Bath being awarded in lieu.

Army Gold Crosses and Medals Introduced in 62 1813 by the Prince Regent on behalf of King George III to commemorate the outstanding victories of the Napoleonic Wars and also the American 1812–14 war. The gold medals were awarded in two sizes. The larger, 2·1 inches in diameter, was restricted to General officers and the smaller, 1·3 inches in diameter, was awarded to officers commanding regiments and battalions. The name of the first action was engraved in the centre of the reverse, although that for Barossa was die-struck. In addition, a small special medal was struck for Maida 1806. A second or third action was covered by die-struck gold bars attached to the riband. Officers who were engaged in more than three actions received a gold cross in lieu, the names of the action appearing on the four arms, with bars on the riband for additional actions.

Altogether, 163 crosses, 85 large and 599 small gold

medals were issued; consequently the larger gold medals are the rarest. After the termination of the Peninsular War, and prior to Waterloo, these awards were discontinued as, by then, the Order of the Bath had been enlarged so as to include a military division with three classes. It became the normal practice to reward distinguished officers with one of these insignia. Unlike Naval Officers who also received the Naval General Service medal in 1848, Army officers did not receive the silver Military General Service medal if they had been awarded a gold cross or medal.

63 Naval General Service, 1793–1840 Although awarded to those who had served in the Napoleonic Wars prior to Waterloo, this medal, like its Army counterpart was not authorized until 1847, and then it was issued only to those *still surviving*. As a result of illiteracy, lack of communication and publicity, many entitled would not have claimed their medals; consequently the numbers issued for some of the approved actions were very few indeed.

The medal was originally intended to cover the period 1793–1815, but the period was extended to 1840 which included the combined British and Dutch attack on Algiers, the attack by the combined fleets of Britain, France and Russia on the Turkish and Egyptian fleets in 1827, and another combined fleet attack on Egypt in 1840.

Almost 24,000 medals were issued, and of these almost 21,000 had a single bar. The maximum number of bars issued with one medal was seven. Five medals had six bars and fourteen medals were awarded with five bars.

The medal awarded to Rear-Admiral Sir George Cockburn had six bars. He was in command in each action, the actions commencing in 1795 and ending in 1813. As a finale to such an active career, including 68 years *continuous* service of which 56 years were afloat,

62 ARMY GOLD CROSS AND
MEDAL
(a) (*right*) reverse,
larger General Officers'
medal

62 (b) (*above*) Gold Cross
with an additional clasp

62 (c) (*right*) obverse,
larger General Officers'
medal

this officer escorted Napoleon to exile on St Helena.

One of the most extraordinary actions for which this medal was awarded was 'Speedy 6th May 1801'. Capt. Lord Cochrane with the little *Speedy*, which carried only 14 four-pounder guns, and a crew of 6 officers and 54 men, chased and boarded the 32-gun Spanish frigate *Gamo* which had a crew of over 300. Laying the *Speedy* alongside, Cochrane boarded the Spaniard with the whole of his crew except for the doctor and two seamen!

63 NAVAL GENERAL SERVICE 1793–1840 reverse, with bar for Trafalgar

It is interesting to note that a medal may have been issued to a woman for participation at Trafalgar and also to a baby born to a Mrs McKenzie during the battle of the Glorious First of June aboard H.M.S. *Tremendous*. He was duly christened Daniel Tremendous McKenzie!

The N.G.S. medal is particularly interesting in that it was issued for actions against France, Holland, Spain,

Denmark, Sweden, Turkey, Egypt, Algiers, U.S.A. and Russia.

64 Military General Service, 1793–1814 As with the Naval General Service medal of the same period, this medal was not authorized until 1847 and was then issued only to the survivors living at that time. Some 25,650 applications were made for the medal, which was awarded with 29 different bars, but the maximum number issued with any one medal was 15 of which two

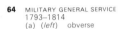

64 MILITARY GENERAL SERVICE
1793–1814
(a) (*left*) obverse

64 (b) (*right*) reverse

were issued; eleven medals were awarded with 14 bars.

The majority awarded were issued to cover Wellington's victories in Spain and Portugal, although bars were issued for places such as Egypt 1801, and the East and West Indies, Italy, and also for the war with the U.S.A. 1812–14. One bar was issued for Fort Detroit, which is the only American place name that has appeared on a British Military medal. Although the medal carries the date 1793, the first action covered by the medal was for Egypt 1801. No doubt the date 1793 crept in as this was the date used for the Naval medal.

It is interesting to note the delay in the approval of this medal, which came about 46 years after the first action. It is said that this was because the Duke of Wellington was opposed to the issue of a medal to all ranks. However, when the medal finally came about he managed to incorporate into the reverse a likeness of himself kneeling before the Queen (Victoria, had come to the throne in the meantime), who is about to place a laurel wreath of victory on the Duke!

65 Army of India Medal, 1799–1826 This was the fourth and last medal (awarded to Europeans and Natives) to cover events connected directly or indirectly with the Napoleonic Wars. An Order authorized the Honourable East India Company to issue a medal some four years after the Naval and Military General Service medals. A similarity occurred with all three medals in that Queen Victoria, whose effigy appeared on all three, was not born when many of the actions were fought! This was not the first medal awarded by the Honourable East India Company as they had made a practice for very many years of issuing medals long before the British Government realized the necessity of issuing such tokens.

The medal is unusual in that the last awarded bar is placed nearest the medal; that is, the correct order or sequence reads downward. One medal was awarded

with as many as seven bars and three received six bars.
These particular medals covered periods of service from
1803 to 1826—a remarkable period if one takes into
account the hardship and conditions of service against
very determined enemies and in an alien climate. The
medal covered three separate wars namely the second
Mahratta War, 1803–4 (the first took place in 1778–84),
the Nepaul War, 1814–16, and the Pindaree or third
Mahratta War, 1817–18. It was in the second Mahratta
war that Major-General Arthur Wellesley (later Duke
of Wellington) made his name as an outstanding General

and tactitian, hence his later nickname of 'the Sepoy General'.

66 **Waterloo, 1815** This was the very first medal as we know it today, which was awarded by the British Government to officers and other ranks alike and which set the pattern for more than 100 campaign medals and 550 bars or clasps issued to date. It is interesting to note that Waterloo ushered in an era of almost 100 years without a major war, and yet in that period we have issued such a large number of medals—for keeping the

66 WATERLOO 1815
(a) (*below*) obverse

66 (b) (*above*) reverse

peace! Although styled as the Waterloo medal, it was awarded to all who had taken part in one or more of the following battles: Ligny, 16 June; Quatre Bras, 16 June and Waterloo, 18 June. Every soldier present was credited with two years extra service.

Owing to the fact that most of the seasoned veterans of the Peninsular War had been disbanded or had been sent to America to fight in the war of 1812–14, Wellington's army of 106,000 contained barely one-third of British troops. The remainder consisted of the King's German Legion, the Hanoverian troops and those from Brunswick, Nassau, Holland and elsewhere. Of this composite force, the cavalry and infantry of the King's German Legion were particularly outstanding in their achievements. One outstanding deed was executed by Colonel Halkett of the Legion who, like a knight in the olden days of chivalry, singled out in the heat of battle and amidst the general carnage, the French General Cambronne, engaged him in single combat and took him prisoner.

Another instance of the attitude of those serving was that of The Marquis of Anglesey. This brilliant leader of Cavalry was wounded in the right knee during the last charge; his leg was amputated after battle and buried under a tree to which a board was erected inscribed, 'Here lies the Marquis of Anglesey's leg. Pray for the rest of his body, I beg'.

Certain regiments at Waterloo suffered extremely heavy casualties and medals awarded to men of these regiments are naturally much sought after. The regiments concerned were certain Cavalry regiments, the Guards Regiments (in particular the 3rd Bn. Grenadier Guards who suffered 604 casualties out of a strength of 1,021), the 42nd and 79th Foot, as well as others.

Burma Medal, 1824 This was the first of the Company's 'modern' smaller size standard medals, issued for wear with a riband 1·5 inches in width.

67 BURMA 1824
(a) obverse   (b) reverse

The obverse depicts the elephant of Ava kneeling before the British lion, with palm trees and the Union Flag; an inscription is contained in the exergue. The reverse contains a scene of the storming of the Pagoda at Rangoon. The medal was awarded to the Bengal and Madras armies, native officers were awarded a gold medal and native troops a silver one. Europeans later received the Army of India medal with the clasp for Ava.

The war was the result of repeated acts of aggression by the Burmese governors on the borders adjacent to the East India Company's territory.

68 Ghuznee Medal, 1839 (21–23 July) Awarded to those who participated in the first of the wars in Afghanistan which was to be a regular battle ground of the armies in India during the next hundred years.

The medal, which shows on the obverse the gate of the Cabul fortress that was blown in, was issued by the Honourable East India Company to both the British and Indian forces; it was struck at the Calcutta mint in 1842. The medal was originally issued with a riband half green and half yellow, but this seems to have been changed at a very early date to half crimson and half green.

The purpose of invading Afghanistan was to dethrone the anti-British Dost Mahomed who had exiled Shah Shujah, as there was a possibility that the new régime might have encouraged Russia to take an active interest in the affairs of Afghanistan. This policy might eventually have endangered the Indian sub-continent. The successful invasion was under the overall command of Sir H. Fame, C.-in-C. in India who had armies from

68 GHUZNEE 1839
obverse

the Bengal and Bombay Presidencies under his direction.

The defeat of the forces of Dost Mahomed enabled Shah Shujah to be reinstated; to record his appreciation, the Shah instituted the Order of the Dooranie Empire, which was awarded in three different classes to British officers of field rank and above.

69 CHINA 1840–2 reverse

69 China War Medal, 5 July 1840—29 August 1842

This medal was originally suggested by the Governor-General of India for presentation to all ranks of the Honourable East India Company's forces. It was, however, subsequently awarded by the Home Government in 1843 to those who had taken part in the capture of the island of Chusan, the operation in Hongchow Bay and in the Canton River during 1841. The campaign ended with the capture of Nangking. The British possession of Hong Kong dates from this period.

The original design of the medal was different from that subsequently issued. The reverse depicted a lion with its forepaws on a dragon with 'NANGKING 1842' in the exergue. Upon reflection this design was considered to be offensive to the Chinese and a trophy of arms design was substituted.

The war itself gradually came about as a result of the vastly different methods of trading adopted by the

British and Chinese merchants. The final breaking-point came when the Chinese destroyed vast quantities of the prohibited drug, opium, of which the Honourable East India Company had the monopoly.

Scinde Campaign Medals, 6 January—24 March 70 1843 Three different strikings of the medal were authorized which differ only as regards their reverses being either 'MEEANEE', 'HYDERABAD' or both 'MEEANEE' and 'HYDERABAD'. Four ships of the Indian Navy took part in the campaign. The 22nd Foot (the Cheshire Regt.) was the only English regiment to which this medal was granted.

70 SCINDE MEDALS 1843
(a) (*left*) reverse,
Meeanee issue

70 (b) (*right*) reverse,
Meeanee, Hyderabad
issue

The withdrawal of the troops from Afghanistan following the First Afghan War was regarded by the Ameer of Scinde as a sign of weakness, and as Scinde was allied to the Dooranie Empire, the Scinde Army opened hostilities.

A force was assembled under Major-General Sir Charles Napier, their first task being the destruction of the Fort of Emaun Ghur, in the desert. This service was described by the past-master of military tactics, The Duke of Wellington, 'as one of the most curious military feats he had ever known to be performed'.

The actions of the Queen's and East India Company's force throughout the campaign so impressed the Governor-General of India that he directed that the captured guns taken at Hyderabad be cast into a triumphal column and be engraved in English and two native languages with the names of the commanding officer, officers, N.C.O.s and men mentioned in the despatches.

General Sir Charles Napier set the example, which has since been more or less followed, in naming in his despatches N.C.O.s and men who had specially distinguished themselves.

71 Gwalior Campaign Stars, December 1843 Bronze stars worn from riband as opposed to medals, were a new introduction, being issued with either 'MAHARAJPOOR' or 'PUNNIAR' superimposed in the silver centre. The stars themselves were struck from the bronze guns captured from the enemy.

Although peace manoeuvres were being carried out so as to overawe the population, events moved swiftly and the exercises quickly changed to war operations with the result that four ladies, who were spectators, came under the fire of the Mahratta guns. Lord Ellenborough, the Governor-General, gave these four ladies gold and enamel stars bearing the Queen's effigy. The two wings of the Army of Gwalior, one under Sir Hugh Gough and the other under Major-General

71 GWALIOR STARS 1843
obverse, Punniar
issue

Grey, fought battles independently of each other at Maharajpoor and Punniar respectively on the same day, 29 December 1843. The regiments that particularly distinguished themselves were Her Majesty's 16th Lancers and the 39th (The Dorsetshire Regt.) and the 40th Regt. (South Lancashire Regt.).

South Africa Medal, 1834–53 Awarded to the sur-   **72** vivors of the three Kaffir wars fought between 1834–5, 1846–7 and 1850–3. As all received the same medal without bars with the date '1853' on the reverse, it is impossible to tell which campaign, or campaigns, a recipient served in.

The campaigns took place because of the aggressive nature of the warlike Kaffir tribes, which were divided into three nations: the Amapondas, the Tambookies and the Amakosa. Frequent raids on the settlers made it necessary for the Commander-in-Chief, Major-General

Sir Benjamin D'Uban (the seaport of Durban is named after him) to assemble a force consisting of British and local troops. The second-in-Command was Sir Harry Smith—later Governor of the Cape Province. (The town of Ladysmith was named after his wife in 1851.)

The second campaign of 1846–7 was more hazardous for the troops as, by then, the natives had acquired firearms with the result that the Army suffered many casualties at Sandilli before the surrender in October 1847.

In 1850 Chief Sandilli again caused trouble by blockading Sir Harry Smith in Fort Cox. The severe fighting caused unexpected setbacks to the British troops, which resulted in the Commander-in-Chief being replaced by Sir George Cathcart. One interesting sidelight was the sinking of the troopship *Birkenhead* off South Africa. The epic gallantry and outstanding discipline of the troops on board so impressed King

72 SOUTH AFRICA 1834–53
reverse

73 NEW ZEALAND 1845–66
(a) (*left*) obverse

73 (b) (*right*) reverse with
dates 1861–1866

William of Prussia that he had the full story read out on
parade in every barracks in Germany.

New Zealand Medal, 1845–7 and 1860–6 This 73
medal is unusual in that the dates of service of the
recipients were die-struck in the centre of the reverse,
with the exception of those issued to members of the
Army for the first of the Maori wars. Owing to casualties and sickness some of the dates are very rare. In
addition to the Royal Navy and the Army, medals were
also awarded to local forces with titles such as Colonial
Force Interpreters, Bay of Island Volunteers and Kai Iwi

89

Volunteer Cavalry. The first uniformed Australians to be engaged in war were the crew of H.M.'s Colonial Steamer *Victoria*, and about 2,000 Australians who served in the Waikato Regiments.

The first British settlers arrived in New Zealand in 1839 and a treaty was concluded with the Maoris regarding the purchase of lands. However, it was not long before the increasing number of settlers placed a strain on relations, with the result that fighting broke out and this did not cease until 21 February 1848, when a general pardon was granted and peace came.

The second Maori war lasted from 1860–6 with an interval of peace for some months. This, like the first war, arose over disputes concerning the sale and possession of land. The Maori tribes proved themselves to be remarkable antagonists, their bravery and strategy causing many British casualties. In the early spring of 1866 peace was declared, and from that time onwards relationships between the proud Maoris and settlers improved, with the result that complete integration has taken place, both nations being equally respected in all walks of life.

74 Candahar, Ghuznee and Cabul Medals, October 1841—October 1842 There were four medals with totally different designs for the first Afghan war, namely Ghuznee 1839 (No. 68), Candahar, Ghuznee and Cabul 1842 (No. 74), Jellalabad 1842 (No. 75) and Khelat-i-Ghilzie 1842 (No. 75).

The four varieties of medals in question all bore on the obverse the diadem head of Queen Victoria with the legend 'VICTORIA VINDEX', while the reverses bore the name of the action, or actions, in cases where a recipient was involved in more than one of the battles. These different reverses read 'CANDAHAR', 'GHUZNEE' and 'CABUL' or 'CANDAHAR, GHUZNEE, CABUL'.

All were suspended from similar ribands (1·75 inches in width) of a rainbow pattern watered red, white, yellow, white and blue, known as 'the military ribbon of India'.

The medals were issued to both the Queen's forces and those of the Company at the expense of the Honourable East India Company. After the fall of Ghuznee, and the conclusion of the 1839 campaign, the army of occupation was largely reduced, the remaining garrison being scattered throughout Afghanistan at Candahar, Kelat-i-Ghilzie, Ghuznee, Cabul and Charikar. Continued desultory fighting had occurred throughout 1840–1, and as the garrison was in the process of being further reduced, ferocious fighting broke out again,

74 CANDAHAR, GHUZNEE & CABUL MEDALS 1841–2 (a) *(left)* reverse, Candahar, Ghuznee, Cabul issue

74 (b) *(right)* reverse, Ghuznee, Cabul issue

sweeping away the garrisons of Cabul, Charikar and Ghuznee, causing Brigadier Sale's brigade to take refuge in Jellalabad. In Southern Afghanistan Kelat-i-Ghilzie held out, and at Candahar, Major-General Nott kept the field the whole winter, even though all communications with India were cut.

The activities of the mobile and warlike Afghans caused the campaign to evolve into a succession of marches and counter marches, defences and reliefs of columns and fortresses through hard winters and hot summers, during which, many regiments particularly distinguished themselves.

The most notable event amongst so many was the virtual annihilation of the 44th Foot, the Essex Regiment. In October 1841 a rebellion against the Shah, who was supported by the British, broke out. The British envoy, Sir William McNaughten, and Sir Alexander Burnes were treacherously murdered, and the troops were compelled to leave Cabul and retreat to Jellalabad, during which they were cut to pieces. Only Dr Bryden managed to reach Jellalabad. The number of the Essex Regiment killed was 565; three officers and 51 men were taken prisoner, 36 of them being later released by British troops.

75 Jellalabad Medal, 12 November 1841—April 1842. Defence of Kelat-i-Ghilzie (February–May 1842)

The events which made it necessary to issue these two medals formed part of the first Afghan war referred to under medal number 74.

The Jellalabad medals were issued to the surviving members of the garrison which gallantly defended the fortress of Jellalabad from 12 November 1841 to 7 April 1842. Later, the medal was extended to the next of kin of those killed, most of these receiving a medal with the Flying figure of Victory on the reverse. (The first medal had the date only on the reverse.)

The Kelat-i-Ghilzie medal is particularly rare as none

75 JELLALABAD, KELAT-I-GHILZIE 1842
(a) (*left*) obverse, Jellalabad first type

75 (b) (*above*) reverse, Jellalabad first type

75 (c) (*left*) obverse, Kelat-i-Ghilzie

of the Queen's regiments was present, although forty European artillery and sixty Sappers and Miners took part.

76 **Sutlej Campaign Medal, 18 December 1845— 22 February 1846** The medal awarded for this campaign was the first with bars to be given to both officers and men. (The medals for the earlier Napoleonic wars were not authorized until 1847.) The first action in which a recipient participated was contained in the reverse exergue so that four different reverse dies were used to cover the four battles. Further actions were recorded by bars attached to the medal. The only Queen's regiments that took part in all four actions were the 31st (East Surrey Regt.) and 50th Foot (Royal Queen's West Kent Regt.). Consequently many men

76 SUTLEJ 1845–6 Moodkee reverse, with three additional engagement bars

of these regiments received the medal with three bars, thus covering the four actions.

A state of anarchy ruled in the Sutlej following the death of the ruler, Runjeet Singh in 1839, which culminated in the Sikh army, some 100,000 strong, crossing the river Sutlej into the East India Company's territory. The Governor-General, Sir H. Hardinge, ordered the concentration of the British troops and promptly marched with them himself! The casualties were particularly severe, which is perhaps not surprising in view of the fighting qualities of the Sikh nation. British regiments suffered 50 per cent casualties to the officers and 40 per cent other ranks in the short period of less than two months. Three Major-Generals and four Brigadiers were killed, and one Major-General and seven Brigadiers were wounded, which shows that commanding officers of those days certainly did not control battles from a safe distance!

To illustrate that campaigns were a 'way of life' in those days, medals were given to Prince Waldemar of Prussia and his suite, six in all, who accompanied the Governor-General in the field as his guests! One of them, Dr Hoffmeister, was killed at Ferozeshuhur.

Punjab Campaign Medal, 7 September 1848— 77
14 March 1849 This campaign was really an extension of the Sutlej campaign (medal No. 76). In spite of, or perhaps because of, their heavy defeats in that campaign the feelings of hatred still persisted among the Sikh population and warriors. This hatred culminated in the murder, in Mooltan, of the British Resident, Mr Vans Agnew and a Lieut. Anderson, which gave the signal for the ruler to recommence hostilities.

Three separate battles took place, these being Mooltan, Chilianwala and Goojerat, bars for these actions being attached to the medal given to those engaged. Otherwise medals were awarded without bars to those not actually involved in fighting.

77 PUNJAB 1848–9
reverse

The reverse of the medal is one of the most attractive ever designed, depicting Major-General Sir Walter Gilbert on horseback, receiving the surrender of the Sikh army, with a palm tree on a hill with an inscription. The celebrated diamond, the Koh-i-Noor, or Mountain of Light, was captured during the campaign and was presented to Queen Victoria. It is now set in the crown for wear by a Queen Consort, which is on permanent display in the Jewel House at the Tower of London.

78 Indian General Service Medal, 1854–95 Instituted in January 1854 to commemorate the campaign in Burma between 28 March 1852 and 30 June 1853. It was decided that, unlike several of the earlier Indian

PLATE 1

The Order of the Bath *(top)* Knight Commander Breast Star and Badge (civil) *(bottom)* Knight Commander Badge and Breast Star (military)

PLATE 2 : RIBBONS No. 1 — No. 24

1 Order of the Garter

2 Order of the Thistle

3 Order of St Patrick

4 Order of the Bath

5 Order of Merit

6 Guelphic Order

7 Order of the Star of India

8 Order of St Michael & St George

9 Order of the Indian Empire

10 Order of the Crown of India

11 Royal Victorian Order

12 Order of the British Empire (civil)

13 Companion of Honour

14 Baronets' Badge

15 Knight's Bachelor Badge

16 Royal Family Orders (E II R issue)

17 Order of Victoria & Albert

18 Order of St John of Jerusalem

19 Victoria Cross

20 New Zealand Cross

21 George Cross

22 Distinguished Service Order

23 Royal Red Cross

24 Distinguished Service Cross

PLATE 3 : RIBBONS No. 25 — No. 48b

25 Military Cross

26 Distinguished Flying Cross

27 Air Force Cross

28 Order of British India

29 Kaiser-I-Hind

30 Albert Medal (2nd class, land)

31 King's (& Queen's) for Bravery (S. Africa)

32 Distinguished Conduct Medal

33 Conspicuous Gallantry Medal (pre 1921)

34 George Medal

35 & 36 King's & Queen's Police & Fire Brigade

37 Queen's Fire Service Medal for Gallantry

38 Edward Medal

39 Indian Distinguished Service Medal

40 Distinguished Service Medal

41 Military Medal

42 Distinguished Flying Medal

43 Air Force Medal

44 Indian Order of Merit (military)

45 Burma Gallantry Medal

46 Sea Gallantry Medal

47 Burma Police Medal

48a Indian Police (pre 1944 General)

48b Indian Police (post 1944 Gallantry)

PLATE 4 : RIBBONS No. 49—No. 80

49 Colonial Police Medal for Gallantry

50 Medal British Empire (military)

51 Medal British Empire (civil)

52-60 Early East India Co. Medals

61 Naval Gold Medal

62 Army Gold Cross and Medal

63 Naval General Service 1793-1840

64 Military General Service 1793-1814

65 Army of India Medal 1799-1826

66 Waterloo 1815

67 Burma Medal 1824

68 Ghuznee Medal 1839

69 China Medal 1842

70 Scinde Campaign Medal 1843

71 Gwalior Campaign Stars 1843

72 South Africa Medal 1834-53

73 New Zealand Medal 1845-66

74 Candahar, Ghuznee & Cabul 1841-2

75 Jellalabad 1841-2, Kelat-I-Ghilzie 1842

76 Sutlej Campaign Medal 1845-6

77 Punjab Campaign Medal 1848-9

78 India General Service Medal 1854-95

79 Baltic Medal 1854-5

80 Crimean War Medal 1854-6

PLATE 5 : RIBBONS No. 81—No. 104

81 Indian Mutiny Medal 1857-8

82 Second China War Medal 1857-60

83 Canada General Service Medal 1866-70

84 Abyssinian War 1867-8

85 Ashantee War Medal 1783-4

86 South Africa Medal 1877-9

87 Second Afghan War Medal 1878-80

88 Kabul to Kandahar Star 1880

89 Cape of Good Hope General Service 1880-97

90 Egyptian Medal 1882-9

91 Khedive's Egyptian Star 1882-91

92 North-West Canada 1885

93 Royal Niger Co's Medal 1886-97

94 East & West Africa Medal 1887-1900

95 British South Africa Co's Medal 1890-7

96 Central Africa 1891-8

97 Hong Kong Plague Medal 1894

98 India General Service 1895-1902

99 Ashanti Star 1896

100 Queen's Sudan Medal 1896-7

101 Khedives' Sudan Medal 1896-1908

102 British N. Borneo Co's Medal 1897-1937

103 East & Central Africa Medal 1897-9

104 Queen's South Africa 1899-1902

PLATE 6 : RIBBONS No. 105—No. 122g

105 King's South Africa Medal 1901-2

106 Ashanti Medal 1900

107 China War Medal 1900

108 Transport Medal 1899-1902

109 Africa General Service 1902-56

110 Tibet Medal 1903-4

111 Natal 1906

112 Indian General Service 1908-35

113 Sudan Medal 1910

114 Naval General Service 1915-64

115 1914 and 1914-15 Stars

116 British War Medal 1914-20

117 Mercantile Marine War Medal 1914-18

118 Victory Medal 1914-18

119 Territorial Force War Medal 1914-19

120 General Service Medal 1918-64

121 Indian General Service 1936-9

122a World War II Star 1939-45

122b World War II Star —Atlantic

122c World War II Star —Air Crew Europe

122d World War II Star —Africa

122e World War II Star —Pacific

122f World War II Star —Burma

122g World War II Star —Italy

PLATE 7 : RIBBONS No. 122h—No. 131b

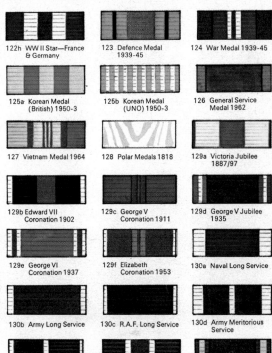

122h WW II Star—France & Germany

123 Defence Medal 1939-45

124 War Medal 1939-45

125a Korean Medal (British) 1950-3

125b Korean Medal (UNO) 1950-3

126 General Service Medal 1962

127 Vietnam Medal 1964

128 Polar Medals 1818

129a Victoria Jubilee 1887/97

129b Edward VII Coronation 1902

129c George V Coronation 1911

129d George V Jubilee 1935

129e George VI Coronation 1937

129f Elizabeth Coronation 1953

130a Naval Long Service

130b Army Long Service

130c R.A.F. Long Service

130d Army Meritorious Service

130e R.A.F. Meritorious Service

131a Army Best Shot

131b Champion Shot R.A.F.

PLATE 8

(top) The Order of St Michael & St George Knight Grand Cross
Breast Star (20th century)   *(centre)* The Order of the British
Empire Commander's Badge (2nd type)   *(bottom)* The Guelphic
Order Knight Grand Cross Star (military) London made pre 1837

medals, the medal would not be issued without a bar. When a recipient qualified for a second or third bar after the issue of the medal, the bar(s) was forwarded and the recipient attached it himself, which explains the unofficial rivets and wrong order in which some bars are placed.

The medal itself is very common, but some of the 23 bars are rare, such as Kachin Hills 1892–3, Hunza 1891 and Chin Hills 1892–3. Kachin Hills 1892–3 awarded to the Yorkshire Regiment and Chin Hills 1892–3 to the Norfolk Regiment are the rarest.

The maximum number of bars to one medal appears to be seven. Commencing with the bar for Burma 1885–7, the medals were also awarded in bronze to camp servants and followers. The 23 bars awarded are: Pegu, Persia, North West Frontier, Umbeyla, Bhootan, Looshai, Perak, Jowaki 1877–8, Naga 1879–80, Burma

78 INDIAN GENERAL
SERVICE 1854–95
reverse

1885–7, Sikkim, Hazara, Burma 1887–9, Chin Lushai 1889–90, Lushai 1889–92, Samana 1891, Hazara 1891, North East Frontier 1891, Hunza 1891, Burma 1889–92, Chin Hills 1892–3, Kachin Hills 1892–3, Waziristan 1894–5.

79 **Baltic Medal, March 1854—August 1855** This medal was sanctioned in 1856, as an award for services in the Baltic under Admiral Sir Charles Napier and Rear-Admiral the Hon. R. Dundas. The British fleet consisting of about 100 ships including floats and mortar ships was reinforced by a French fleet. The combined fleets then engaged the forts at Hango Head, attacked Cronstadt and destroyed Russian merchant ships in the Gulfs of Bothnia and Riga. Bomarsund was also attacked; Sappers and Miners who had embarked with the fleet, landed for the purpose of demolishing the forts. During August 1855 Captain Lyons (son of Admiral

79 BALTIC 1854–5
reverse

Lyons, later Naval Commander-in-Chief, Crimea) entered the White Sea and attacked Kola. The port of Petropaulouski in the north-east of Russia was also attacked.

Later, in March 1858, another fleet was sent to the Baltic. Sveaborg was attacked and Helsingfors (now called Helsinki) was practically burnt out.

The reverse of the medal in question shows the seated figure of Britannia. Behind her are depicted the fortresses of Bormarsund and Sveaborg.

Crimean War Medal, 29 March 1854—30 March 1856

Queen Victoria was so stirred by the deeds performed by her army in the Crimea that she directed that a medal be issued in 1854 with bars for Alma and Inkermann, which explains why the single date 1854 is contained on the obverse. Bars for Balaklava and Sebastopol were not sanctioned until the following year. A few of the medals were awarded to our French allies.

The war with Russia came about for a number of reasons, but perhaps the overriding reason from the British point of view was the need to contain Russia within her boundaries and to prevent her from expanding into Turkey, then known as 'the sick man of Europe'. On 28 May 1854, Britain and France declared war on Russia; they were joined later on by the Italian kingdom of Sardinia.

The epic gallantry and extreme suffering of the troops during the campaign are part and parcel of our history, and reflect the fact that the armed forces were ill prepared to combat the hardships and climate that prevailed.

Many are the deeds of outstanding bravery and devotion to duty. It is impossible to record all of them here, but the immortal charge of the Light Brigade under Lord Cardigan, the charge of the Heavy Brigade under General Scarlet, and the activities of Florence Nightin-

80 (b) (*above*) obverse.
Turkish medal to British
forces

80 CRIMEA 1854-6
(a) (*left*) reverse.
British medal

gale who nursed the sick and wounded and who
influenced nursing practice thereafter, should be mentioned. The army was led by many Generals whose last
active service was under Wellington, in the Napoleonic
Wars, and it is recorded that Lord Raglan the Commander-in-Chief often referred, unthinkingly, to the
French as 'the enemy'!

The Turkish Government awarded a service medal
to their allies, approval being given by the British
Government for this to be worn while in uniform.

The obverse includes a cannon and a mortar with crossed flags of Turkey and her allies with wording and '1855' in the exergue. The arrangement of the allied flags and spelling of 'Crimea' depended on which country the particular medal was intended for. As the medals seem to have been awarded indiscriminately they are found with 'CRIMEA 1855' 'LA CRIMÉE 1855'—French issue, or 'LA CRIMEA 1855'—Sardinian issue.

Indian Mutiny Medal, 1857-8 This was the last of the medals issued by the Honourable East India Company, as the authority of the Company over its domains was transferred to the Crown in 1858, although Queen Victoria was not proclaimed Empress of India until 1877. During the period from 1778 when the Company issued its first medal (though not alike to officers and men) it was responsible for numerous fine medals,

81 INDIAN MUTINY 1857–8
reverse

and also for setting the 'fashion' and pattern for the British Government from 1816 onwards.

The medal in question was awarded with five different bars, namely: Delhi, Defence of Lucknow, Relief of Lucknow, Lucknow and Central India, although the maximum number issued on one medal was four. Fewer than 200 were awarded to the Bengal Artillery. The maximum number of bars given to the Queen's troops was three; these were awarded to those of the 9th Lancers who qualified.

Unrest among some of the Indian princes and the population had been fermenting for many years, the final breaking-point probably being caused as a result of the actions of the Indian Government who had practically disposed of the power of the Kings of Oude and Delhi. In turn these sovereigns encouraged the Mutiny by means of rumour and propaganda.

Medals to the 32nd (Duke of Cornwall's) Light Infantry are particularly prized by collectors for the part they played throughout the Defence of Lucknow. Those awarded to the Naval Brigade who were employed in no fewer than 10 battles throughout India in its fifteen months of existence are also much sought after.

82 Second China War Medal, 1857–60 The second China war arose from various aggressive acts by the Chinese, amongst which the seizure of the crew of the *Arrow*, sailing under British colours, was the most prominent. The operations were at first confined to the Navy and the Marines under Admiral Sir Michael Seymour who pursued vigorous measures in Fatshan Creek in June 1857. Eleven British gunboats and about 50 ships and boats defeated 80 junks armed with 800 guns and manned by 6,000 seamen.

Having defeated the fleet, no further operations could be undertaken except the capture of Canton by seamen and the only British Regiment on the spot, the 59th

82 CHINA 1857–60
obverse

(E. Lancashire) Regt.   Peace was then signed on 26 June 1858; the troops sent out from the United Kingdom in the meantime were diverted to quell the Mutiny in India.   The signature of a treaty was one thing, the ratification another.   When the British envoy was proceeding up the Peiho River the forts at the mouth of the river opened fire upon the ships accompanying the Envoy and it was therefore decided that a force of arms should be employed.

An army of 10,000 British and a force of 7,000 French was organized, a joint operation which, with co-ordination, finally defeated the Chinese and resulted in the capture of the Taku Forts, 1860, and the occupation of Pekin.   The Pekin Summer Palace was destroyed by fire, an operation which took two days, and indiscriminate looting took place; the troops had no idea of the value of the gems of art and wonderful pieces of jewellery and jade.

The medal was approved on the 28 February 1861, being awarded either without a bar or with a bar or bars for China 1842, Fatshan 1857, Canton 1857, Taku Forts 1858, Taku Forts 1860, Pekin 1860. The bars for Fatshan 1857 and Taku Forts 1858 were awarded only to the Naval forces.

83 **Canada General Service Medal, 1866-70** An Army order as late as January 1899 gave approval for the Canadian Government to issue a medal (some 30 years after the event) to both the British forces and the Canadian local forces for participation in the Rebellions of 1866 and 1870. Altogether 17,600 were awarded, 15,300 of them going to Canadians and 2,300 only to the British Army and Navy. The rarest of the three bars is that for Red River 1870, fewer than 400 being issued; only 23 medals contained all three bars. The campaign took place after the end of the American Civil War when large numbers of soldiers were available for recruitment. The Fenians, whose aims were to cause Britain embarrassment by trying to establish a united Irish Republic, organized an invasion of Canada from the United States. At the town of Ridgeway the force defeated a unit of the Canadian Militia, but then retreated across the border where many were arrested.

In 1870 the Fenians again crossed over the border, this time into Manitoba, but without success. Shortly afterwards the territories of the Hudson Bay, on the expiry of their charter, were incorporated into the State of Manitoba. This caused resentment in many people and a certain Louis Riel styled himself a General, seized the Hudson Bay Company's treasury and imprisoned many residents. Colonel (later Lord) Wolseley's expedition of over 1,100 miles to Fort Garry (Winnipeg) was accomplished in record time, law and order soon being restored after a period of unrest which could have resulted in a permanent break-away state being founded within Canada.

83 CANADA GENERAL SERVICE 1866–70 reverse

Abyssinian War, 1867–8 The medal, which was **84** sanctioned on 1 March 1869, is said to be the most expensive of the general issue campaign medals, because the recipients' names were embossed in the reverse centre, thus necessitating a separate name die for each medal. Those awarded to the Indian troops, however, had their names impressed in the more normal way, this detail being in the centre of the reverse.

Some 12,000 medals were awarded to the British Army and 2,000 to the Royal Navy who fought under Lt.-Gen. Sir Robert Napier (later Lord Napier of Magdala). This campaign is not as well known as the

Crimea and Indian Mutiny. This is probably due to the
fact that it was one of the most successful ever fought, the
casualties amounting to only two killed and 27 wounded.
As a result of the lack of blood and thunder it has always
failed to attract the publicity that less successful campaigns have gained. It could be that the Italians were
influenced by our success when they embarked on a
similar expedition in 1896. Then their forces suffered
almost total annihilation at Adowa!

The war of 1867–8 was the result of King Theodore's
imprisoning of the British Consul, other British subjects
and foreigners. After negotiations, the prisoners were
released, but within a short time they were rearrested

together with the negotiators! The campaign caused
the capital of those days, Magdala, to be captured and
razed to the ground; the King committed suicide and
peace terms were concluded.

Ashantee War Medal, 9 June 1783—4 February 85
1874 Awarded for Major-General Sir Garnet Wolseley's campaign against King Coffee Kalkali, who resented
the transfer of the port of Elmina from the Dutch to the
British. The Dutch had made a practice of giving
King Coffee an annual payment for the use of the port;
this ceased when the British took over, which would
explain the King's reasons for being antagonistic.

During the early part of the campaign, the fighting
on the coast was undertaken by a small force of Marines
and the Royal Navy. The advance on, and the capture
of Coomassie (spelt Kumassi on the 1900 campaign
medal) was not undertaken until 5 January 1874, and

85 ASHANTEE 1873–4
reverse

was completed by 4 February, during which period four Victoria Crosses were won. Captain Glover with a small naval detachment and local forces known as 'Glover's Force' was detailed to take Coomassie in the rear, a move which forced King Coffee to pay the indemnity demanded by General Wolseley. The rate of sickness was extremely high during the campaign; in fact some 98 per cent of the naval force engaged on land reported sick during the period.

The medal was issued with a bar for Coomassie, this bar being awarded to those who advanced on the capital. The reverse of the medal incorporates a pleasing departure from previous designs in that it shows bush fighting, with a native in a half lying position. Medals awarded to natives recruited locally by the Navy are sometimes found officially inscribed with the somewhat amusing names given to them by the crews, such as Peasoup, Bottle of Beer, Prince of Wales and Tom Twoglass.

86 **South Africa Medal, 25 September 1877—2 December 1879** This was issued to cover the Zulu and Basuto wars. The medal was exactly the same as that for the earlier wars fought between 1835 and 1853 except that the reverse date, 1853, was replaced by a Zulu shield and four crossed assegais. The medal, unlike its predecessor, was issued with a date bar as follows: 1877, 1877–8, 1878, 1878–9, 1877–8–9 and 1879.

During 1877 the Galeka and Gaikas tribes attacked the Fingoes, a tribe which was under British protection. This act was punished by a force composed of the Army, with local units and a naval brigade, all under Lt.-Gen. Sir Arthur Cunyinghame. Further fighting took place during 1878 against the Pokwane and Griqua tribes, but the most notable and disastrous events came about at the end of 1878 and the beginning of 1879. King Cetewayo of the Zulu nation proved an outstanding foe, and Dambulamanzi, his half-brother, attacked

Lord Chelmsford's columns near the border at Isandhl-
wana; more than 1,300 British troops, including the
24th Foot (The South Wales Borderers), and native
followers were annihilated. On the same night,
flushed with success, the Zulus moved on some 10 miles
to the post at Rorkes Drift. Here the small garrison of
139 men who were guarding the sick and wounded

86 SOUTH AFRICA 1877–9
reverse

were attacked by 3,000 Zulus. During the epic defence
(the subject of an outstanding film entitled 'Zulu'), the
garrison under Lieutenants Bromhead and Chard, won
no fewer than 11 Victoria Crosses. The campaign
came to an end following the successful battle at
Ulundi.

Second Afghan War Medal, 1878–80 The medal, **87**
which shows on the reverse a striking scene of troops

on the march with an elephant carrying a gun, was awarded with a variety of six different bars. The maximum number of bars to one medal was four, the details of the six bars being: Ali Musjid, Peiwar Kotal, Charasia, Ahmed Khel, Kabul and Kandahar. The medal was awarded in silver to the troops, both British and Indian, but the camp followers received theirs in bronze; these are rare.

The Amir of Afghanistan in 1873 agreed on the thorny question of boundaries between Afghanistan and India, and the maintenance of peace for which he was paid a subsidy. In 1877 Shere Ali refused to accept a British Resident at Kabul and raised an army to antagonize the British forces stationed on the border. In 1878 he signed a treaty with Russia giving her the guardianship

87 AFGHAN 1878–80
reverse

of himself and the right to protect Afghanistan which, at that time caused the British Government to fear for the safety of their Indian possessions. The war that followed, directed by General Roberts, was a particularly difficult campaign owing to the type of country and the warlike Afghans. During the war, in July 1879, Sir Louis Cavagnari was appointed Resident at Kabul, but on 3 September Sir Louis and his staff, together with his bodyguard of the Corps of Guides, were murdered.

The action fought at Maiwand by the 66th Regiment (2nd Bn. Royal Berkshires) and E. Battery, B. Brigade of the Royal Horse Artillery was one of the most outstanding actions in the annals of the British Army, medals to these two units being rather more valuable. The total casualties in the whole war were just over 2,250 of which 1,150 were incurred at the battle of Maiwand.

Kabul to Kandahar Star, 9–31 August 1880 This 88 award was a departure from the more normal silver medals, being star shaped and in bronze; the metal used was taken from the captured guns. The reverse is plain, apart from the recipient's rank, initials, name and unit which were impressed; those awarded to the native regiments were engraved. The stars were struck by H. Jenkins & Sons of Birmingham and occasionally specimens are found either unnamed or with the maker's name on the reverse. These are naturally not so highly prized—or priced—as those awarded to participants. The star was issued in conjunction with the silver medal having the Kandahar bar, and was awarded to those who had taken part in General Roberts' famous march of just over 300 miles from the capital of Kabul to relieve the garrison at Kandahar, the British and Indian armies having a total strength of 9,560, comprising 2,560 British and just over 7,000 native troops, with 18 guns.

General Roberts, having relieved the garrison,

88 KABUL TO KANDAHAR 1880
obverse

attacked the enemy encamped in the vicinity who were
flushed with their victory at Maiwand. Using the
same tactics as in the earlier actions, the enemy were
defeated within an hour and, as a result, the war finally
came to a halt although the border area could never be
described as peaceful.

89 Cape of Good Hope General Service Medal, 1880–97

The medal, issued with the arms of Cape
Colony on the reverse, was awarded with one or more
bars: Transkei (13 September 1880–27 April 1881),
Basutoland (13 September 1880–27 April 1881) and
Bechuanaland (24 December 1896–30 July 1897); only
thirteen medals were issued with all three bars. The
medal was awarded by the Cape Government in 1900
for services in suppressing small risings in the places

mentioned above. The disturbances broke out for several reasons. The first was caused by the defeat of Chief Moirosi (for which the South Africa Medal 1877–9 was issued) and the peace terms which dictated that all arms were to be handed in. These, however, were not obeyed and were resented by the natives; consequently, not long afterwards the settlers were being attacked again. Another cause was a serious outbreak of disease among the cattle in Bechuanaland which led to the slaughter of large numbers of cattle; this the natives naturally resented.

89 CAPE OF GOOD HOPE
1880–97
(a) (*left*) obverse

89 (b) (*right*) reverse

The medals were all awarded to local regular and volunteer regiments. British regiments did not participate.

90 **Egyptian Medal, 1882–9** The obverse of this medal contains the diadem head of Queen Victoria and a legend; the reverse contains an appropriate Sphinx on a pedestal with the word 'EGYPT' above. Those awarded for the first campaign contained the date '1882' in the exergue, while those awarded for the later campaign were undated. The riband, of blue and white stripes, is significant of the Blue and White Niles.

The maximum number of bars issued with one medal was seven, but only one was awarded. Six were issued with six bars; medals with five bars are rare, while those with four are not common.

The strategic position of Egypt from the British point of view was made even more important by the opening of the Suez Canal in 1869. Owing to the general financial chaos that prevailed, the Egyptian army were not paid and as a result mutinied; matters deteriorated and the Arabs attacked the Europeans. In May 1882 a British and French squadron of warships arrived at Alexandria and as ultimatums demanding law and order went unheeded, the forts at Alexandria were attacked and destroyed, and the canal seized by a combined force of the British Army and Navy, the French having decided to withdraw from the conflict.

In 1884, further south in the Sudan, a Mahdi, or self-proclaimed God, raised a force which annihilated the Egyptian troops and this caused another combined British operation. General Gordon in command of the garrison at Khartoum was besieged, the British forces failing to relieve him prior to he and his garrison being overwhelmed. Egypt and the Sudan were not pacified until August 1889, following the battle of Toski. Medals awarded to the few Canadian boatmen are particularly rare. These boatmen were recruited

90 EGYPT 1882–9
reverse

from the various provinces in Canada for their particular skill and experience in shooting rapids, being of especial value in transporting the Army and its supplies up the river Nile. An interesting aspect of the campaign was that Thomas Cook, the travel agent, was commissioned by the Government to convey parts of the Army, and its stores up and down the Nile.

Khedive's Egyptian Star, 1882–91 Issued by the Khedive of Egypt, being authorized by His Imperial Majesty the Sultan of the Ottoman Empire, in appreciation of the services rendered by the British Army and Navy. The star, in bronze, depicts in the centre a Sphinx with three pyramids behind. Around the

91 EGYPT STAR 1882–91
(a) (*left*) obverse

91 (b) (*right*) reverse

centre is a circle with the word 'EGYPT' followed by the appropriate date or dates. The reverse is plain apart from the Khedive's monogram in the centre. The stars were made by Henry Jenkins & Son of Birmingham.

There were four issues of the star to correspond with the different campaigns:

Dated 1882 for operations between 16 July and 14 September.

Dated 1884 for operations between 19 February and 26 March.

Dated 1884–6 for operations between 26 March 1884 and 7 October 1886.

Undated for operations near Suakin in 1887 and on the Nile in 1889. Later extended for the action at Tokar in 1891. Recipients of the undated star for this action received a clasp for Tokar.

North West Canada, 1885 Although the medal for the earlier campaigns of 1866–70 was not issued until 1899, the medal in question was authorized earlier by the Canadian Government, in 1885. No British troops were engaged apart from 16 Officers who were on the staff in Canada at that time. In all, just over 5,600 medals were awarded, these being unnamed, although a number of recipients did have their medals privately named. The medals were issued with a bar for Saskatchewan to those who took part in the three main encounters, but just occasionally an unofficial bar is found for Bartoche, where 850 men were engaged. In addition to the troops, 34 men of the steamer *Northcote* were

92 NORTH WEST CANADA 1885
reverse

awarded the medal.   An interesting aspect was that the Order which sanctioned the medal also awarded to each soldier, except the North-West Mounted Police, a grant of 320 acres of land or $80 script in lieu.

This campaign came about indirectly, owing to the construction of the Canadian Pacific Railway, which opened the prairies to white settlers, thus presenting a threat to the M'etis, or half-breeds, who squatted on much of the land likely to be granted to the new settlers.

Representations were made to the Government by the half-breeds, but as the Government had failed to agree, Louis Riel formed a provisional Government at Bartoche.   Riel, it will be recalled, was the ring-leader during the 1866–70 period, but after his capture he escaped in 1870 from Fort Garry.   The operation lasted from 24 April to the 28 May 1885, during which the rebels were quickly defeated, Riel being captured and hanged.

93   ROYAL NIGER
COMPANY 1886–97
obverse

Royal Niger Company's Medal, 1886–97 The obverse of the silver and bronze medals contains the crowned and veiled head of Queen Victoria and a legend, while the reverse incorporates a shield with 'PAX, JUS, ARS', arranged in the form of a Y with two flags above. The whole is surrounded by a wreath of laurel. The medal was designed and struck by the London company of Spink & Son Ltd.

The silver medals, awarded to Europeans, are named while the bronze medals to natives were impressed with the recipient's number only. A bar reading 'NIGERIA 1886–97' was issued with the silver medal, and one reading 'NIGERIA' for the bronze.

In 1899 the Company (Chartered as the Royal Niger Company in 1866) had its charter revoked and the territory of present-day Nigeria was taken over by the Imperial Government. Fewer than 100 medals were awarded in silver to officers and N.C.O.s, for numerous small expeditions against tribes such as the Lapai and Argeyes.

East and West Africa Medal, 1887–1900 The medal and its ribbon is identical to the Ashantee Campaign medal 1873–4 (No. 85), except that the medal is slightly thinner. Twenty-two different bars were awarded; it could not be awarded without at least one bar, except for Mwele 1895–6. This action was commemorated by the name and date of the campaign impressed on the edge, which was a unique departure from normal practice. The medal is occasionally found in bronze. No medals were awarded to British Regiments as a whole, although officers and N.C.O.s seconded to native regiments have their parent regiment impressed on the medal rim. Many of the bars, however, were awarded to the Royal Navy whose ships were very active off the coasts and in the many rivers.

The medal is another in the 'general' series, in that it was issued for numerous small punitive campaigns and expedition over a period. Perhaps the most curious incident was the transportation of the *Adventure* and *Pioneer*, which were hauled in sections over 200 miles of virgin country to be assembled on Lake Nyassa.

The undermentioned 23 bars were issued, of which those for Liwondi 1893, Juba River 1893, Lake Nyassa and Dawkita 1897 are the rarest.

1887–8	1896–7
Witu 1890	1896–8
1891–2	Niger 1897
1892	Benin 1897
Witu August 1893	Dawkita 1897
Liwondi 1893	1897–98
Juba River 1893	1898
Lake Nyassa 1893	Sierra Leone 1898–9
1893–94	1896–9
Gambia 1894	1899
Benin River 1894	1900
Brass River 1895	

95 British South Africa Company's Medal, 1890–7

The reverse of this striking medal depicts a charging lion with a spear sticking in its chest. In the background is a mimosa bush, and in the foreground is a native shield and spears. Above are the name and date of the campaign for which the medal was first issued, and below 'BRITISH SOUTH AFRICA COMPANY'.

Four different bars were issued for those that took part in more than one campaign, namely Mashonaland 1890, Matabeleland 1893, Rhodesia 1896 and Mashonaland 1897.

The Queen sanctioned the issue by the British South Africa Company in 1899. In 1927 a similar medal was issued to recognize services in Mashonaland in 1890; it carried no place, name or date on the reverse and is the rarest of all the issues. Four men were entitled to the medal, with four bars, but only one is known to have been issued. Twelve medals were awarded with three

94 EAST AND WEST AFRICA
1887–1900
reverse

95 BRITISH SOUTH AFRICA
COMPANY 1890–7
reverse, Rhodesia issue

bars. Medals were issued to Imperial troops and also to local units, the medal with the reverse reading 'RHODESIA 1896' is the commonest issue.

96 **Central Africa Medal, 1891–8** This is one of several medals issued for service in and around Africa during the latter half of the 19th century, during the period when the different spheres of European interest were taking shape.

The medal was issued for two occasions: firstly in 1895 to commemorate ten small campaigns in Central Africa between 1891 and 1894, and again in 1899, for several more in the same geographical location. The first period produced a medal with a swivel ring suspender and no bar; for those engaged in the second phase of operations a suspender bar was added with a clasp reading 'CENTRAL AFRICA 1894–98'. These are quite scarce. The medals were mostly awarded in silver,

96 CENTRAL AFRICA 1891–8
reverse

122

although just a few were issued in bronze. The riband is divided into three equal stripes of black, white and terracotta, representing the African, British and Indian troops engaged.

Hong Kong Plague Medal, 1894 Although the **97** medal was not authorized to be worn in uniform, owing to the very lax regulations of the period it is quite feasible that the medal was worn, especially as groups mounted for wear are sometimes found with the medal.

The obverse of this interesting medal shows a Chinaman lying on a trestle table, his head supported by the right arm of a soldier who, with his left arm is fending off a winged figure of death. A European nurse is bending over the other side of the table.

The reverse reads 'FOR SERVICES RENDERED DURING THE PLAGUE OF 1894: PRESENTED BY THE HONG KONG COMMUNITY'. This medal was given by the Hong

97 HONG KONG PLAGUE 1894 obverse

Kong Community to 300 men of the 85th Foot (Shropshire Light Infantry) and some 50 members of the Royal Navy and Royal Engineers, as well as to the local police.

In April 1894 a severe epidemic of bubonic plague broke out near Canton and in May gained a foothold in Hong Kong. Over 2,500 people died during a three-month period. Civilians and armed forces provided valuable assistance in nursing, as well as work in isolating and disinfecting houses. Medals were awarded in silver, although almost 50 were awarded in gold to officers and those whose assistance had been particularly outstanding.

98 Indian General Service, 1895–1902 Owing to the

98 INDIAN GENERAL SERVICE
1895–1902
reverse

fact that a total of 23 different bars had been issued with the 1854–95 medal, there came about a need for an entirely new medal.

The medal was issued with two different obverses. The first bore the crowned and veiled head of Queen Victoria and the legend 'VICTORIA REGINA ET IMPERATRIX'. The second, the head and shoulders of Edward VII in Field Marshal's uniform. The reverse shows a British and a native soldier both supporting the same standard. On the left is the word 'INDIA' and on the right the date '1895'. The Edward VII issue had the date removed.

Six bars were issued: Defence of Chitral 1895, Relief of Chitral 1895, Punjab Frontier 1897–8, Malakand 1897, Samana 1897, Tirah 1897–8 and Waziristan 1901–2 (this bar was issued with the Edward VII obverse, unless the recipient had qualified in one of the earlier campaigns, in which case the bar was attached to his existing Victorian medal). The rarest bar is that for Defence of Chitral, followed by Malakand. Unlike the earlier medal for 1854–95, all issues were awarded in silver *and* bronze. They were issued to British and Indian regiments but not to the Royal Navy.

Ashanti Star, 1896 This unusual looking bronze 99 medal is in the form of a four-pointed star together with the cross of St Andrew. The raised centre contains a crown surrounded by 'ASHANTI: 1896' The simple reverse contains the wording 'FROM THE QUEEN'. When originally issued they were of dull bronze; it is said that the star was designed by Princess Henry of Battenberg, whose husband died of fever in the campaign. All were issued unnamed except those to the West Yorkshire Regiment, the Colonel having the medals to the 2nd Battalion named at his own expense.

In 1895 trouble in Ashanti necessitated the sending of a small force, comprising the 2nd Battalion of the West Yorkshire Regiment, and a composite battalion made up of 20 men from each of the Grenadier, Cold-

99 ASHANTI STAR 1896
obverse

stream and Scots Guards Regiments, and eight regiments of the line, as well as the supporting forces of the Artillery and Engineers. The total strength of the force was approximately 2,000 and was under the command of Major-General Sir F. C. Scott. The campaign culminated in the capture of the capital Coomassie (now part of Ghana).

100 **Queen's Sudan Medal, 1896–7** Issued in 1899 in both silver and bronze, both without bars. The obverse depicts Queen Victoria, whilst the reverse shows a fine figure of Victory who is seated holding a palm branch in her right hand and laurel wreath in her left. At her feet is the word 'SUDAN' and behind are the British and Egyptian flags.

The medal was awarded to those engaged in the reconquest of the Sudan (which followed our departure some years before), and the final overthrow of the followers of the Mahdi, the Egyptian army having in the meantime been made into a disciplined force by their British officers.

The actions covered by the Queen's medal include that at Khartoum, which was the central stronghold of the enemy. This action was known as the Battle of Omdurman where the British 21st Lancers made their gallant charge against a very large and determined enemy force. Some 500 casualties were incurred by the British, but the enemy suffered 10,000 in dead alone. As a result the Khedive of Egypt's rule was restored in the Sudanese provinces. Medals to the 21st Lancers are the most valued.

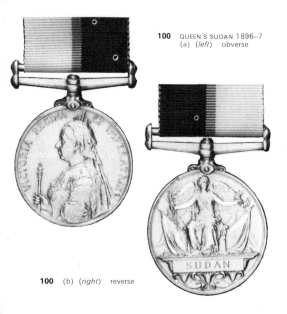

100 QUEEN'S SUDAN 1896–7
(a) (*left*) obverse

100 (b) (*right*) reverse

101 Khedive's Sudan Medal, 1896–1908 Sanctioned by an Egyptian Army Order in 1897 to commemorate the recapture of the Dongala Province and then extended for later campaigns. It was awarded to both the British and the Egyptian armies, as well as to the Royal Navy, the medal being scarce to British troops with more than two bars (i.e. those for Atbara and Khartoum). Occasionally the medal is found without a bar in bronze. Fifteen different bars were issued, the maximum number being ten (to Egyptian troops and their British officers). As the medal could measure up to 7 inches in length in cases where there were many bars, it made the wearing of multiple bars rather difficult!

The riband is sand in colour, representing the desert, with a central blue stripe for the river Nile.

1937 This is one of the series of medals issued by a 'trading' company such as those awarded by the Honourable East India Company, the Royal Niger Company and others. The medals were issued in silver and bronze (except Rundum, which was in silver only) to British and native officials, servants and a small number of Sikh troops. British subjects were not permitted to wear the medal except in Borneo. The bars awarded were

102 BRITISH NORTH BORNEO COMPANY 1897–1937
(a) (*left*) obverse, Tambunan issue

102 (b) (*right*) obverse, Punitive Expedition issue

Punitive Expedition (1897), Punitive Expeditions (1898), Tambunan (1899–1900) and Rundum (1915–16). In addition, a General Service medal without bar was issued in 1937.

The medals were struck by Spink & Son Ltd. of London.

103 **East and Central Africa Medal, 1897–9** The obverse contains the half-length figure of Queen Victoria wearing a small crown and veil with the legend 'VICTORIA REGINA ET IMPERATRIX'. The reverse shows the standing figure of Britannia holding a trident in her right hand and an olive branch and scroll in her left hand. Behind her is a figure of the British Lion, with a rising sun. In the exergue is 'EAST AND CENTRAL AFRICA'.

Four bars were issued: Lubwa's, Uganda 1897–8, 1898 and Uganda 1899; none was awarded without a

103 EAST AND CENTRAL AFRICA 1897–9 reverse

bar. That for Lubwa's was only issued as a 2-bar medal, which was normally Uganda 1897-8.

Lubwa's was awarded for service against 500 Sudanese troops who had refused to undertake a mission. Uganda 1897-8 was for an expedition under Lt.-Col. W. A. Broome into the Teita country. 1898 was awarded for service in the Ogaden area against the Somalis, and Uganda 1899 was awarded to a force which advanced down the Nile and captured Kabarega and M'Wanga in the Uganda Protectorate.

The medal was awarded to African and Indian Regiments, but not to British Units as a whole.

Queen's South Africa Medal, 1899-1902 Awarded 104 to the Navy, Army (including local troops) and certain civilians employed in official capacities for quelling the uprising of the Boers. The first medals struck contained on the reverse the dates '1899-1900' in relief. These

104 QUEEN'S SOUTH AFRICA
1899-1902
(a) obverse

104 QUEEN'S SOUTH AFRICA
1899–1902
(b) reverse

were issued to Lord Strathcona's Horse, a Canadian unit, the medals being hastily prepared so that they could be presented at Buckingham Palace while the unit was in the United Kingdom in transit for Canada. It was then realized that the period of the war was extending beyond 1900, consequently all further issues had the dates removed, although 'ghost' dates can just be seen on some of the post-1900 medals.

Medals of the first issue with raised dates are rare, as are those with the bars for the Defence of Mafeking, and to a lesser extent, Defence of Kimberley, Wepener and Rhodesia. The maximum number of bars issued to any one medal was nine to the Army and eight to the Navy. The medals were issued to a very wide variety of units of which some were employed for the first time in a theatre of war; these included the Balloon and

Photographic sections, the Cyclist units, the Field Force Canteen, as well as units from Canada, Australia, New Zealand and numerous volunteer battalions from the British Isles. Medals without bars were awarded in bronze to local natives and Indian troops. Medals with no bar but with 'MEDITERRANEAN' on the reverse were awarded to the third battalions of certain British Regiments who guarded Boer prisoners on the island of St Helena.

King's South Africa Medal, 1901–2 The obverse 105 contains the bust of King Edward VII, the reverse being the same as the Queen's medal. This issue was never awarded without the Queen's Medal, neither was it issued without a bar except to nurses who were awarded almost six hundred medals. King Edward VII authorized the medal to be given to all who were serving in South Africa on or after 1 January 1902, and who would

105 KING'S SOUTH AFRICA
1901–02
reverse

complete eighteen months' service before 1 June 1902. Very few of the King's medals were awarded to the Royal Navy as the Naval Brigades returned to their ships in 1901. Thirty only were awarded to Canadians.

106 Ashanti War Medal, 31 March—25 December 1900 This medal, the first sanctioned by King Edward VII, shows on the reverse the British Lion facing left and standing on a rock and below, a native shield and two assegais. The word 'ASHANTI' appears at the base with a rising sun to the left. Only one bar was awarded, namely Kumassi (note the difference in spellings between the earlier medal for Ashantee and bar for Coomassie).

The medal was awarded in silver and bronze (mostly to the native carriers) to West African troops only. At that time the Boer war was placing heavy demands on the Imperial troops, and none could be spared to combat the Ashanti uprising.

106 ASHANTI 1900 reverse

This is the third and last of the medals awarded for services against China (unless we consider the Naval General Service medal with bar for Yangtze), the previous medals being for 1842 and 1857–60. The reverse is the same as that for the second war of 1857–60 except that the date 1900 has been inserted; the riband is also similar.

107 CHINA 1900 reverse

Three bars were issued, namely Taku Forts, Defence of Legations and Relief of Pekin, two bars being the maximum issued with any one medal. Most of the medals were issued in silver, but native servants and followers received theirs in bronze.

The war, known as the Boxer Rebellion, followed the persecution of European missionaries and traders by the various Chinese secret societies which the Chinese

Government were not able or willing to curtail. The Royal Navy began hostilities in June, under Admiral Sir Edward Seymour, but as various European trading interests were involved, an international force was assembled, comprising in the main, British, American, French, Japanese, Russian, and German troops under the overall command of the German Field-Marshal Count Van Waldersee. The most spectacular or well-known event was the defence and relief of the allied legations in Pekin. As a result, medals with the bar Defence of Legations are far more valuable than the others issued.

108 **Transport Medal, 1899–1902** The medal was the first ever introduced for award to the Mercantile Marine (the only other was that for the 1914–18 War), but it is unusual in that it was not awarded to all. It was restrict-

108 TRANSPORT 1899–1902 reverse

ed to the Master, 1st, 2nd and 3rd Officers, 1st, 2nd and 3rd Engineers, Pursers and Surgeons only of Merchant vessels employed in the Transport Service which took troops to South Africa and/or China; medals were also awarded to the 11 hospital ships. 1,270 medals were awarded with the bar 'S. Africa 1899–1902', 323 with bar 'China 1900' and 188 with both bars.

The obverse of the medal depicts the effigy of King Edward VII in naval uniform and the reverse shows H.M. Transport *Ophir*, with a map of the world and the Latin inscription 'OB PATRIAM MILITIBUS PER MARE TRANSVECTIS ADJUTAM'.

109 AFRICA GENERAL SERVICE 1902–56 reverse

Africa General Service Medal, 1902–56 Sanctioned **109** in 1902 to replace the East and West Africa Medal to which 22 bars had already been awarded. During the lifetime of the medal, extending over a period of 54 years (the longest survival rating of all British Service medals) with a span of 36 years between the last two bars, the medal was issued with the obverse effigies of Kings Edward VII and George V, and Queen Elizabeth II (no bars were awarded during the reign of King George VI 1936–52). The reverse is virtually the same as the East and Central Africa medal with a standing figure of Britannia, but the wording in the exergue 'EAST AND CENTRAL AFRICA' was replaced by 'AFRICA'.

Thirty-four bars were awarded with the Edward VII obverse, ten with the George V and one only with that of Queen Elizabeth II—a total of 45.

The medal was awarded in silver, but a few were issued in bronze, these being without a bar or with the bars for Somaliland 1902–4 or Somaliland 1908–10. These bronze issues are scarce, as indeed are all issues with the head of George V. Over such a long period it is natural to find that some of the actions commemorated were very minor affairs, whilst others such as those for Somaliland and Kenya involved a very considerable number of troops, police and even civilians.

110 **Tibet Medal, 13 December 1903—23 September 1904** Authorized on 1 February 1905 for award to all who took part in the Tibet Mission and to the troops accompanying it who served at or beyond Silgari. The medals were awarded in bronze to the Peshawar Camel Corps and native camp servants with or without the bar Gyantse. The majority of the silver medals were earned by Indian Regiments; those to the few British regiments are rather scarce on the market.

The obverse contains the bust of King Edward VII, and the reverse the fortress of Potala Lhassa with 'TIBET 1903–4'. In July 1903 a trade mission, under Colonel Younghusband, was sent by the Indian Government to Tibet but its progress was barred by hostile

Tibetan troops.   As a result, heavy fighting occurred in and around Gyantse.   A treaty was eventually signed by Colonel Younghusband at Lhassa.

110 TIBET 1903–4
reverse

Natal, 8 February—3 August 1906 The obverse **111** shows the usual effigy of Edward VII while the reverse contains, in the centre, the figures of Britannia and Natalia.   The former holds an orb while Natalia holds a large sword in her right hand.   The word 'NATAL' appears in the exergue.

The medal was issued without a bar, but the majority received a medal with a bar reading '1906'; the medal was issued only in silver.   Those who served for from 20 to 49 days received the medal without the bar, while those who served for 50 or more days received the medal with bar.

The cause of the rebellion was the natives' refusal to

139

pay taxes which was followed by the murder of two
Natal policemen.   The Natal Government organized a
number of attacks which quickly achieved the desired
results.   No Imperial troops were present, all those who
took part being from local units including the Natal
Naval Corps whose members received altogether about
200 medals.   One interesting recipient was Sergeant-
Major M. K. Ghandi of later fame, elected as a National leader of the independent State of India, he had
previously been responsible for guiding India towards
independence.   Unfortunately, he was assassinated in
1948.

112 **Indian General Service Medal, 1908–35** This is
the fourth of the Indian General Service medals and it
was sanctioned by King Edward VII.   Twelve different
bars were issued during the reigns of Kings Edward VII
and George V.   The medals with the bars North

112 INDIAN GENERAL SERVICE 1908–35 reverse

West Frontier 1908 and Abor 1911–12 were awarded in silver *and* bronze, while the remaining issues were in silver only.

The reverse shows the fort at Jamrud which commands the Khyber Pass eleven miles from Peshawur. Three different obverses were used: Edward VII with the bar for North West Frontier 1908; George V with the legend 'GEORGIUS V KAISER-I-HIND' for the bars Abor 1911–12, Afghanistan N.W.F. 1919, Mahsud 1919–20, Waziristan 1919–21, Malabar 1921–2, Waziristan 1921–4 and Waziristan 1925; George V with the legend 'GEORGIUS V.D.G. BRITT. OMN. REG. ET. INDIAE. IMP' with the bars North West Frontier 1930–1, Burma 1930–2, Mohmand 1933 and North West Frontier 1935.

Medals were struck by the Royal Mint in London and by the Indian Government Mint in Calcutta, the only

141

difference being a slight variation in the claws. Most of the bars are quite common, with the exception of Abor 1911–12, Mahsud 1919–20, Malabar 1921–2, Waziristan 1925 and Mohmand 1933, when awarded to British Forces, especially the Royal Air Force.

113 **Sudan Medal, 1910** As with the medal for Sudan 1896–1908, this was awarded by the Khedive of Egypt. The obverse incorporates an Arabic inscription which reads 'ABBAS HILMI THE SECOND' with the Mohammedan year of 1328 for those awarded from 1910 to 1917; those from 1918–1922 contained the cypher of the new Khedive. The reverse shows a lion standing on a plinth which is inscribed with the word 'SUDAN' in English; behind the lion is the river Nile, with palm trees and a rising sun. The recipients of the medals were mainly Egyptian or Sudanese troops, but a few British officers and men of the R.A.S.C. and R.A.F., as well as those serving with the Khedive's forces seconded from the British Army, received the medal. Sixteen different bars, each of which is inscribed in English and Arabic were issued. The medal was awarded in silver and bronze, although the scarce bronze medals were awarded without a bar; all were awarded unnamed.

The medal was awarded for the general pacification of the Sudan, including expeditions as far south as the Abyssinian border. The bars issued were: Atwot, S. Kordofan 1910, Sudan 1912, Zeraf 1913–14, Mandal, Miri, Mongalla 1915–16, Darfur 1916, Fasher, Lau Nuer, Nyima 1917–18, Atwot 1918, Garjak Nuer, Aliab Dinka, Nyala, Darfur 1921.

114 **Naval General Service, 1915–64** This is the second General Service medal issued to the Navy, the earlier one being predominantly for the Napoleonic Wars from 1793. The medal was issued with the effigies of Kings George V and VI, and also Queen Elizabeth II, five different obverses being issued in all. The reverse

113 SUDAN 1910
(a) (*left*) obverse

114 (*above*) NAVAL
GENERAL SERVICE
1915–64
reverse

113 (b) (*left*) reverse

contained Britannia on two sea horses, with her left hand resting on the Union Shield.

The medal was instituted to avoid having to issue a separate medal for the numerous operations in which the Royal Navy and Royal Marines might be involved, but excluding Africa and India as these regions were already covered by the Africa and India Service medals. The first medal issued contained the bar Persian Gulf 1909–14 which was followed by Iraq 1919–20, N.W. Persia 1920, Palestine 1936–9, S.E. Asia 1945–8, Minesweeping 1945–51, Palestine 1945–8, Malaya, Yangtze 1949, Bomb and Mine Clearance 1945–53, Cyprus, Near East, Arabian Peninsula, Bomb & Mine Clearance Mediterranean and Brunei.

Bars for Iraq 1919–20, N.W. Persia 1920, Yangtze 1949, Bomb and Mine Clearance 1945–53, and Bomb and Mine Clearance, Mediterranean are all scarce, especially N.W. Persia 1920. The bar for Yangtze 1949 is perhaps the best-known incident for which the medal was given. H.M.S. *Amethyst* was ordered up the river Yangtze to relieve H.M.S. *Consort*, and to take supplies to the British community, but on her way up she was heavily shelled by the Communist Forces and temporarily driven ashore with 17 killed and 10 wounded. The cruiser H.M.S. *London*, the frigate *Black Swan* and H.M.S. *Consort* failed to relieve her, and as the supplies of the *Amethyst* were becoming very low after a period of 100 days detention with the crew on half rations, Lt.-Comdr. Kerans, her relief captain decided to make a dash down river past the enemy strong points, which resulted in the famous signal being sent by *Amethyst*, 'have rejoined the fleet. No damage or casualties. God save the King.'

115 **1914 and 1914–15 Stars** These were the first of the several medals awarded for the First World War, three distinct types of this star being issued. The first, approved in 1917, was the 1914 Star for award to those

who served in France and Belgium on the strength of a unit between 5 August and midnight on 22/23 November 1914; fewer than 400,000 were awarded. However, in October 1919, King George V sanctioned the award of a bar to the 1914 Star to all who had been under fire in France and Belgium between the above-mentioned dates. The bars, sewn onto the riband of the medal carried '5 AUG.–22 NOV. 1914'; the bar was represented on the tunic by a silver rosette. The majority of the recipients would have been the pre-war regular Army or the 'Old Contemptibles', a term derived from the

115 1914 AND 1914–15
STARS
(a) (*left*) obverse,
1914 issue

115 (b) (*right*) obverse,
1914/15 issue

Kaiser's reference to the British Army as 'the contemptible little army'. The third type is known as the 1914–15 Star which is identical to the 1914 Star except that the central scroll bar bears the dates '1914–15' instead of '5 AUG.–22 NOV. 1914'. This 1914–15 Star was awarded to those who saw service in *any* theatre of war between the 5 August 1914 and 31 December 1915, except those who qualified for the 1914 Star; all were issued in bronze. The plain reverses carry the number, rank, initials, surname and unit of the recipient, the names of the British and Commonwealth units being very varied, which make an interesting collecting and study sphere for the younger collector.

116 **British War Medal, 1914–20** The obverse contains the coinage head of King George V with a legend surrounding, while the reverse shows St George on horseback, the horse being in the process of trampling on the shield of the Central Powers. At the foot is a skull and crossbones with a rising sun above. Around the edge are the dates '1914' and '1918'.

Originally the idea was to award bars to commemorate participation in different battles. 79 were suggested by the Army and 68 by the Navy, but as about 6,500,000 medals were earned, the idea of bars had to be dropped on account of the huge expense. However, the Naval bars were actually authorized but not issued, which explains why miniatures to Naval recipients are sometimes seen with bars.

The medal awarded in silver commemorated some of the most terrible battles ever known, the casualties being astronomical. Some 110,000 medals were awarded in bronze to Chinese, Maltese and other native Labour corps.

The medal was also awarded for post-First World War service in Russia for the period 1919–20, and for mine clearance in the North Sea up to the end of November 1919.

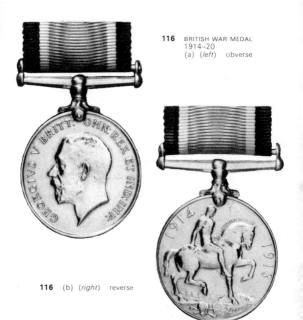

116 BRITISH WAR MEDAL
1914–20
(a) (*left*) obverse

116 (b) (*right*) reverse

Mercantile Marine War Medal, 1914–18   The ob-   117
verse contains the coinage head of King George V with
the usual legend surrounding.   The reverse shows the
bows of a steamship with a sailing ship in the background.   In the foreground is a sinking submarine.
In the exergue the inscription 'FOR WAR SERVICE MER-
CANTILE MARINE 1914–18'.   The riband of green and
red divided by a narrow central white stripe represents
the steaming lights of a ship.

This medal, in bronze, was issued by the Board of
Trade and was awarded to members of the Mercantile

Marine who undertook one or more voyages through a danger zone. Unlike the earlier Merchant Navy medals for the third China and Boer Wars given in silver to officers, this medal was awarded to all, in bronze. Those who completed the whole of their service in the Merchant Navy received this medal and the British War Medal, but the Mercantile Marine medal is often found with the 1914 or 1914–15 Star and Victory medal awarded to those who also served in other units. Just over 133,000 medals were issued.

117 MERCANTILE MARINE 1914–18 reverse

118 Victory Medal, 1914–18 Often called the 'Allied Victory medal', as the same basic design and riband was adopted by Belgium, Brazil (an extremely rare medal), Cuba, Czechoslovakia, France, Greece, Italy, Japan, Portugal, Roumania, Siam, Union of South Africa and the U.S.A. However, in the case of Japan the winged

figure of Victory on the obverse was replaced by a war-rior holding a spear.

The medal was issued in bronze to all those who re-ceived the 1914 or 1914–15 Stars, and to most of those who were awarded the British War medal; it was never awarded singly. To qualify, one had to be mobilized in any of the services between 5 August 1914 and 11 November 1918. Women qualified for this and the earlier two medals, for service with the various nursing and women's auxiliary forces. Those mentioned in dispatches wore an oak leaf on the riband. The reverse contained the inscription 'THE GREAT WAR FOR CIVILIZA-TION 1914–1919' within an oak wreath. The inscrip-tion of those awarded by the South African Govern-ment is in both English and Afrikaans.

Territorial Force War Medal, 1914–19 This is the rarest of the five medals awarded for the First World

119

War, only 34,000 being issued. The bronze medal contained the coinage head of King George V and the usual legend, while the reverse read 'TERRITORIAL WAR MEDAL, FOR VOLUNTARY SERVICE OVERSEAS, 1914–19'. It was awarded to all members of the Territorial Force, including Nursing Sisters, who were members of the service on 4 August 1914, and to those who had completed four years service before that date. In addition, they must have (a) undertaken on, or before 30 September 1914 to serve outside the United Kingdom, (b) to have actually served outside the United Kingdom between 4 August 1914 and 11 November 1918, and (c) been ineligible for either the 1914 or 1914–15 Stars.

120 **The General Service Medal, 1918–64** Awarded to the Army and Royal Air Force (the Navy's general service medal was already in existence, No. 114) for the

numerous actions which fell short of actual war but they did not include any service in Africa or India as the Africa G.S. 1902 and Indian G.S. 1908 medals already covered these spheres. Six different obverses are found with this medal which was awarded with the effigies of Kings George V and George VI, and Queen Elizabeth II. The reverse depicts a standing winged figure of Victory who is placing a wreath on the emblems of the two services.

Sixteen bars were awarded: S. Persia (1918–19), Kurdistan (1919–23), Iraq (1919–20), N.W. Persia (1920), Southern Desert Iraq (1928), Northern Kurdistan (1932), Palestine (1936–9), S.E. Asia 1945–6, Bomb and Mine Clearance 1945–9, Bomb and Mine Clearance 1945–56, Palestine 1945–8, Malaya (1948–1960), Cyprus (1959), Near East (1956), Arabian Peninsula (1957–60) and Brunei (1962). All the bars are quite common with

120 GENERAL SERVICE 1918–64 reverse

the exception of Southern Desert Iraq, Northern Kurdistan, and the two Bomb and Mine Clearance bars.

121 **Indian General Service, 1936–9** The fifth and final of the Indian General Service medals, the earlier ones being: Army of India 1799–1826 (No. 65), India General Service 1854–95 (No. 78), 1895–1902 (No. 98) and

121 INDIAN GENERAL SERVICE 1936–9 reverse

1908–35 (No. 112). As the Second World War commenced in 1939, followed by the partition of the Indian sub-continent, only two bars were issued with this medal—the shortest lived of all the Indian series of general service medals. The bars were for the North West Frontier 1936–7 and North West Frontier 1937–9.

The obverse includes the crowned head of George VI

whilst the reverse includes a tiger with raised right front paws standing on rocky ground with the word 'INDIA' above. As with the previous Indian Medal, this was struck at the Royal Mint in London as well as by the Indian Government Mint in Calcutta, the most noticeable difference being the shoulders to the claws. The Royal Mint issue was quite artistic, but the Indian issue is plain.

The medal and clasp for North West Frontier 1937–9 was not struck and distributed until after the Second World War. This post-war issue did not have a swivelling suspender clasp.

Second World War Campaign Stars 1939–45 122

These campaign stars were all identical in design being six-pointed stars with the crowned cypher of King George VI in the centre. However, the central cypher is partly surrounded by the name of the appropriate campaign, namely '1939–45, ATLANTIC, AIR CREW EUROPE, AFRICA, PACIFIC, BURMA, ITALY, FRANCE/GERMANY'. Unlike the First World War medals, the bronze stars were issued unnamed.

It was laid down that the maximum number of stars that could be earned by one man (or woman) was five. Those who qualified for more received a clasp to the riband, only one clasp to a riband being allowed. Consequently the stars could carry the following clasps:

  a **1939–45**—Battle of Britain
  b **Atlantic**—Air Crew Europe *or* France & Germany
  c **Air Crew Europe**—Atlantic *or* France & Germany
  d **Africa**—North Africa 1940–43 (Naval), *or* 8th Army *or* 1st Army
  e **Pacific**—Burma
  f **Burma**—Pacific
  g **Italy**—None
  h **France & Germany**—Atlantic *or* Air Crew Europe.

122 SECOND WORLD WAR
STARS 1939–45
(a) (*left*) obverse,
1939/45 Star

122 (b) (*above*) obverse,
Air Crew Europe Star

122 (c) (*left*) obverse,
Africa Star

1945 This was the commonest of the Second World War series of campaign or service medals, being awarded to the armed forces and also civilians who formed part of the recognized units such as the Home Guard or Civil Defence. Generally speaking the medal was awarded for three years service at home or for six months' overseas service in a non-operational area which was subjected to, or closely threatened by, air attack. The medal contained the uncrowned effigy of King George VI with the usual legend, whilst the reverse illustrated the Royal Crown resting on the stump of an oak tree flanked by two lions with '1939 1945' at the top and in the exergue 'THE DEFENCE MEDAL'.

It was awarded unnamed, in cupro-nickel, although the Canadian issue was in silver. The riband is very symbolical, the green representing the British Isles, the

123 DEFENCE 1939—45
reverse

orange flames the bombing, and the black, the black-out.

124 The War Medal, 3 September 1939—2 September 1945 Like the Defence Medal, this was also issued in cupro-nickel, although the Canadian issue is in silver. This medal was awarded to all full-time personnel of the Armed Forces wherever they were serving, provided that the duration was at least 28 days irrespective of whether they were operational or non-operational.

124 WAR MEDAL 1939—45 reverse

The obverse included the crowned head of King George VI with the usual legend surrounding, while the reverse contained a lion standing on a dragon that is lying on its back.

125 The Korean Medals (British and the United Nations issues), 2 July 1950—10 June 1953 After

125 KOREAN 1950–3 (a) (*left*) obverse, British issue (b) (*centre*) obverse, United Nation's issue (c) (*right*) Territorial & Auxiliary Volunteer Reserve Decoration (See No. 130)

the conclusion of the Second World War the peninsula of Korea was divided into two countries. The Northern part was under Communist control and the Southern under American influence or protection. The controlling powers withdrew their forces, after which the North attacked the South, which caused the United Nations to intervene with armed forces drawn from a variety of different countries, but chiefly the U.S.A. Great Britain and the Commonwealth countries made a sizeable contribution which resulted in an issue of cupro-nickel medals incorporating the Queen's effigy on the obverse and Hercules, armed with a dagger, with his left hand holding Hydra on the reverse. The word

'KOREA' appears in the exergue. However, Canada issued medals in silver, the obverse legend incorporating the word 'CANADA'. The Union of South Africa issued its own medal, these being quite scarce as only about 800 were issued. The U.N.O. issue was in bronze and the same medal was awarded to all the U.N. troops, except that the reverse inscription was in the language of the country in question.

Medals issued to the 28th Regiment (The Gloucesters) are particularly sought after, owing to this regiment's outstanding action at Hill 235 by the Injim river in April 1951. Of 750 men in the 1st Battalion, only 40 were able to fight their way to their own lines; 150 held on to the hill until relieved, the remaining 560 being either killed or captured by the Chinese army.

126 General Service Medal, 1962– This is the last of the whole series of general service medals and is still being issued. The medal was instituted by the Ministry of Defence in 1964 to replace the Naval General Service Medal 1915 and the General Service Medal 1918 (Army & Royal Air Force). To date six bars have been awarded: Borneo (24 December 1962—11 August 1966) for service against rebel forces in Sabah, Sarawak and Brunei; Radfan (25 April—31 July 1964) for service in the South Arabian Federation; South Arabia (1 August—30 November 1967) for supporting the local government against insurgent forces; Malay Peninsula (17 August 1964—11 August 1966) for efforts during the confrontation with Indonesia; South Vietnam (24 December 1962—29 May 1964) for award to Australian forces only (the U.K. were not at war in S. Vietnam); Northern Ireland (from August 1969) for participation in peace-keeping/police duties. The obverse of the medal contains the crowned effigy of Queen Elizabeth II with legend and the reverse 'FOR CAMPAIGN SERVICE', surrounded by a wreath, and a crown.

127 Vietnam Medals, 1964 British forces have not been

126 (*left*) GENERAL SERVICE 1962 reverse

127 VIETNAM 1964
(a) (*above*) obverse,
South Vietnam issue

127 (b) (*left*) obverse,
Australian & New
Zealand issue

involved in this war. The medals were issued to the armed forces and accredited relief societies of Australia and New Zealand, and were announced in the Government of Australia's gazette of 4 July 1968 and the New Zealand Gazette of 8 August 1968.

The obverse incorporates the crowned bust of Queen Elizabeth II, with a legend surrounding. The reverse, a figure of a nude male pushing one spherical shape from another, represents the parting of opposing forces.

The Government of Vietnam also issued an award to participants in the same way as the U.N.O.s award of a bronze medal for Korea. The Vietnam award is in the form of a six-pointed white enamel star with red enamel flames in the angles, the centre containing a map of Vietnam.

MISCELLANEOUS MEDALS

Polar Medals 1818– This series is perhaps less well **128**
known than the other series of British service medals
and yet they are a fascinating series representing human
endeavour against an enemy as old as time, namely, the
atrocious weather and conditions in both the Arctic
and Antarctic.

The first medal issued was authorized in 1857, this
being an octagonal medal awarded for expeditions of
discovery to the North Pole and for the search for the
North-west Passage to the Far East from 1818 onwards

128 ARCTIC 1818–55
reverse

as well as the searches made for the lost Franklin Expedition of 1845–8.

The second medal was a circular silver medal for award to the crews of H.M.S. *Alert* and *Discovery*, and the yacht *Pandora*, for an attempt to reach the North Pole and to proceed through the North–west Passage 1875–6.

In 1904 a third medal was sanctioned; it was octagonal in shape and is still being currently issued. The first expedition awarded this medal was Captain Scott's first expedition to the Antarctic, followed by Sir Ernest Shackleton's expedition of 1907–9 and then Scott's last fateful expedition from 1910–13. Since then the medals have been regularly issued to the numerous members of expeditions and scientific bases that are constantly manned in the Antarctic. Up to 1939 the medal was awarded in silver and bronze, but is now given only in silver. In 1945 a rosette was authorized for wear on the riband to denote the award of a second bar.

Needless to say Polar medals are scarce and valuable with the exception of the first issue 1818–55.

129 **Jubilee and Coronation Medals, 1887–1953** From the coronation of King Edward VII in 1547 to the coronation of King George VI in 1937, the Royal Mint has always struck official commemorative medallions for general sale to the public, but these were not designed to be worn. However, since Queen Victoria's fiftieth Jubilee in 1887 medals were struck for wear from ribands, being issued to members of the Royal Household, Officers of State, Government Officials, Civil Servants, Members of the Armed Forces on duty as well as selected members of regiments generally. They were also issued to Lord Mayors, Mayors, local government officials and foreigners representing their country in Westminster Abbey. Not only did the medals commemorate the state occasion in London, but also the official visits that followed to Scotland, Ireland and India.

129 JUBILEE & CORONATION
MEDALS
(a) obverse, Victoria
Jubilee 1887 with 1897
Jubilee bar

129 (b) obverse, George V
Jubilee 1935

This series of medals has to date, included:

Queen Victoria
Empress of India Medal, 1877
Jubilee Medal, 1887
    Metropolitan Police
    City of London Police
    Police Ambulance Service
Jubilee, 1887 with 1897 bar
    Metropolitan Police
    City of London Police
    Police Ambulance Service
Jubilee, 1897
    Lord Mayor's issue
    Metropolitan Police
    City of London Police
    Police Ambulance Service
    St John Ambulance Brigade
Visit to Ireland, 1900

King Edward VII
Coronation, 1902
Mayor's issue
Metropolitan Police
City of London Police
L.C.C. Metropolitan Fire Brigade
St John Ambulance Brigade
County and Borough Police
Police Ambulance Service
Delhi Durbar, 1903
Scottish Police, 1903
Visit to Ireland, 1903

129 (c) obverse,
Edward VII Delhi
Durbar 1903

King George V
Coronation 1911
City of London Police
Metropolitan Police
County & Borough Police
London Fire Brigade
Royal Irish Constabulary
Scottish Police
St Andrew's Ambulance Corps
St John Ambulance Brigade

129 (d) (*right*)
obverse, Edward
VII Coronation
1902

129 (e) (*above*)
reverse, Edward
VII Coronation
1902

129 (f) (*left*) reverse,
Edward VII 1902,
Metropolitan Police
issue

129 (h) (*below*)
reverse, George V
Coronation 1911

129 (g) (*right*)
obverse, George V
Coronation 1911

Royal Parks
Police Ambulance Service
Visit to Ireland, 1911
Delhi Durbar, 1911
Jubilee, 1935

King George VI Coronation, 1937
Queen Elizabeth II Coronation, 1953

Up until the Delhi Durbar in 1911 the medals were struck in gold for members of the Royal Family and principal overseas representatives; in silver to officers, and in bronze to other ranks, since when all have been in silver.

129 (i) (*right*)
obverse, George VI
Coronation 1937

129 (k) (*below*)
obverse,
Elizabeth II
Coronation 1953

129 (j) (*above*)
reverse, George VI
Coronation 1937

Long, Meritorious Service and Good Conduct 130
Medals These have been awarded since 1830 by the Army and 1831 by the Navy, followed later by other units such as the Militia, Volunteers, Imperial Yeomanry, Naval Volunteers and others, both at home and in the Dominions and Colonies. The result is that there are a very great variety of different issues, most having numerous different effigies and cyphers, with the result that this series by itself could be a fascinating one for the younger collector, especially as the majority are available for comparatively little money.

The majority, when seen, are virtually self-explanatory, and as they are a series which would need a complete volume to describe in detail, let it be said that the majority of the recipients of the long service medals of the regular forces are likely to have been in receipt also of campaign medals which might be worth looking for.

Prior to the first official government service medal in 1830 it was often the practice of commanding officers of regiments to award medals themselves, as a reward for long or meritorious service; these were often individually hand engraved.

130 (c) (*left*) reverse, R.A.F. Long Service & Good Conduct

130 (d) (*below*) early unofficial engraved Reward of Merit

131 Good Shooting Medals When one considers that the main intention of a soldier in action has always been to shoot the opposing enemy before being shot himself, it is quite natural that medals would have been issued for good shooting, although the official government issues are awarded very sparingly indeed.

The Royal Navy instituted their medal in 1903, but it was discontinued in 1914, the Army in 1869 to 1882, which was revised in 1923. The Queen's medal for Champion Shots of the Air Forces was founded as late as 1953. However, long before 1869, medals were often issued by officers commanding regular regiments or the hastily raised volunteer regiments during the Napoleonic period. These were usually individually designed, many of them being fine examples of the engraver's art.

131 GOOD SHOOTING MEDALS
(a) early unofficial engraved examples

(b) (*above*) reverse
Army Best Shot

THE ORDER IN WHICH ORDERS, DECORATIONS AND MEDALS SHOULD BE WORN

Footnotes are grouped together on pp. 177–179

The following list shows the order in which Orders, Decorations and Medals should be worn. It in no way affects the precedence conferred by the Statutes of certain Orders upon the Members thereof.

Victoria Cross
George Cross
BRITISH ORDERS OF KNIGHTHOOD, ETC.
    Order of the Garter[1]||
    Order of the Thistle[1]||
    Order of St Patrick[1]||
    Order of the Bath||
    Order of Merit[2]|| (immediately after Knights Grand Cross of the Order of the Bath)
    Order of the Star of India||
    Order of St Michael and St George||
    Order of the Indian Empire||
    Order of the Crown of India[3]||
    Royal Victorian Order (Classes I, II and III)||
    Order of the British Empire (Classes I, II and III)[4]||
    Order of the Companions of Honour[2]|| (immediately after Knights and Dames Grand Cross of the Order of the British Empire)
    Distinguished Service Order||
    Royal Victorian Order (Class IV)||
    Order of the British Empire (Class IV)[4]||
    Imperial Service Order||
    Royal Victorian Order (Class V)||
    Order of the British Empire (Class V)[4]||

Note   *The above applies to those Orders of similar grades. When the miniature or riband of a higher grade of a junior Order is worn with that of a lower grade of a senior Order, the higher grade miniature or riband should come first, e.g., the miniature or riband of a K.B.E. will come before a C.B. and a G.C.M.G. before a K.C.B. The ribands of Orders, when the riband alone is worn, will be of the width of the ribands of the Membership of the Order. If there is no Membership Class the riband will be of the width of the riband of the Companionship of the Order.*

BARONET'S BADGE|| || (The Badge is worn suspended round the neck by the riband in the same manner as the neck badge of an Order and takes precedence immediately after the Badge of the Order of Merit. It is not worn in miniature and the riband is not worn with Undress Uniform.)

KNIGHT BACHELOR'S BADGE (The Badge is worn after the Knight Commander of the Order of the British Empire.)
Indian Order of Merit (Military)[5]||

DECORATIONS
Royal Red Cross (Class I)||
Distinguished Service Cross||
Military Cross||
Distinguished Flying Cross||
Air Force Cross||
Royal Red Cross (Class II)||
Order of British India||
Kaiser-i-Hind Medal
Order of St John
Albert Medal||

MEDALS FOR GALLANTRY AND DISTINGUISHED CONDUCT
Union of South Africa Queen's Medal for Bravery, in Gold
Distinguished Conduct Medal||
Conspicuous Gallantry Medal||
George Medal||
Queen's Police Medal, for Gallantry
Queen's Fire Service Medal, for Gallantry
Edward Medal||
Royal West African Frontier Force Distinguished Conduct Medal||
King's African Rifles Distinguished Conduct Medal||
Indian Distinguished Service Medal||
Union of South Africa Queen's Medal for Bravery, in Silver
Distinguished Service Medal||
Military Medal||
Distinguished Flying Medal||

171

Air Force Medal||
Constabulary Medal (Ireland)
Medal for Saving Life at Sea[6]||
Indian Order of Merit (Civil)[7]||
Indian Police Medal for Gallantry
Ceylon Police Medal for Gallantry
Sierra Leone Police Medal for Gallantry
Sierra Leone Fire Brigades Medal for Gallantry
Colonial Police Medal for Gallantry

British Empire Medal[8]||
Canada Medal||
Queen's Police Medal, for Distinguished Service
Queen's Fire Service Medal, for Distinguished Service
Queen's Medal for Chiefs
WAR MEDALS (in order of date of campaign for which
    awarded)[9]
POLAR MEDALS (in order of date)
Royal Victorian Medal (Gold, Silver and Bronze)
Imperial Service Medal

POLICE MEDALS FOR VALUABLE SERVICES
    Indian Police Medal for Meritorious Service
    Ceylon Police Medal for Merit
    Sierra Leone Police Medal for Meritorious Service
    Sierra Leone Fire Brigades Medal for Meritorious Service
    Colonial Police Medal for Meritorious Service[10]
Badge of Honour

JUBILEE, CORONATION AND DURBAR MEDALS
    Queen Victoria's Jubilee Medal, 1887 (Gold, Silver and
        Bronze)
    Queen Victoria's Police Jubilee Medal, 1887
    Queen Victoria's Jubilee Medal, 1897 (Gold, Silver and
        Bronze)
    Queen Victoria's Police Jubilee Medal, 1897
    Queen Victoria's Commemoration Medal, 1900 (Ireland)
    King Edward VII's Coronation Medal, 1902
    King Edward VII's Police Coronation Medal, 1902
    King Edward VII's Durbar Medal, 1903 (Gold, Silver and
        Bronze)
    King Edward VII's Police Medal, 1903 (Scotland)
    King's Visit Commemoration Medal, 1903 (Ireland)
    King George V's Coronation Medal, 1911

172

King George V's Police Coronation Medal, 1911
King's Visit Police Commemoration Medal, 1911 (Ireland)
King George V's Durbar Medal, 1911 (Gold,[11] Silver and Bronze)
King George V's Silver Jubilee Medal, 1935
King George VI's Coronation Medal, 1937
Queen Elizabeth's Coronation Medal, 1953
King George V's Long and Faithful Service Medal
King George VI's Long and Faithful Service Medal
Queen Elizabeth II's Long and Faithful Service Medal

EFFICIENCY AND LONG SERVICE DECORATIONS AND MEDALS
Long Service and Good Conduct Medal
Naval Long Service and Good Conduct Medal
Medal for Meritorious Service‖ ‖
Indian Long Service and Good Conduct Medal (for Europeans of Indian Army)
Indian Meritorious Service Medal (for Europeans of Indian Army)
Royal Marine Meritorious Service Medal
Royal Air Force Meritorious Service Medal
Royal Air Force Long Service and Good Conduct Medal
Indian Long Service and Good Conduct Medal (for Indian Army)
Royal West African Frontier Force Long Service and Good Conduct Medal
Royal Sierra Leone Military Forces Long Service and Good Conduct Medal
King's African Rifles Long Service and Good Conduct Medal
Indian Meritorious Service Medal (for Indian Army)
Police Long Service and Good Conduct Medal
Fire Brigade Long Service and Good Conduct Medal
African Police Medal for Meritorious Service
Royal Canadian Mounted Police Long Service Medal
Ceylon Police Long Service Medal
Ceylon Fire Services Long Service Medal
Sierra Leone Police Long Service Medal
Colonial Police Long Service Medal
Sierra Leone Fire Brigade Long Service Medal
Colonial Fire Brigades Long Service Medal
Colonial Prison Service Medal
Army Emergency Reserve Decoration‖

Volunteer Officer's Decoration||
Volunteer Long Service Medal
Volunteer Officers' Decoration (for India and the Colonies)||
Volunteer Long Service Medal (for India and the Colonies)
Colonial Auxiliary Forces Officers' Decoration||
Colonial Auxiliary Forces Long Service Medal
Medal for Good Shooting (Naval)
Militia Long Service Medal
Imperial Yeomanry Long Service Medal
Territorial Decoration||
Efficiency Decoration||
Territorial Efficiency Medal
Efficiency Medal
Special Reserve Long Service and Good Conduct Medal
Decoration for Officers of the Royal Naval Reserve||
Decoration for Officers of the Royal Naval Volunteer
    Reserve||
Royal Naval Reserve Long Service and Good Conduct
    Medal
Royal Naval Volunteer Reserve Long Service and Good
    Conduct Medal
Royal Naval Auxiliary Sick Berth Reserve Long Service
    and Good Conduct Medal
Royal Fleet Reserve Long Service and Good Conduct
    Medal
Royal Naval Wireless Auxiliary Reserve Long Service and
    Good Conduct Medal
Air Efficiency Award
Queen's Medal (for Champion Shots in the New Zealand
    Naval Forces)
Queen's Medal (for Champion Shots in the Military Forces)
Queen's Medal (for Champion Shots of the Air Forces)
Cadet Forces Medal
Coast Life Saving Corps Long Service Medal[12]
Special Constabulary Long Service Medal
Canadian Forces Decoration||
Royal Observer Corps Medal
Civil Defence Long Service Medal
Union of South Africa Commemoration Medal
Indian Independence Medal[13]
Pakistan Medal
Ceylon Armed Services Inauguration Medal

Ceylon Police Independence Medal (1948)
Sierra Leone Independence Medal
Jamaica Independence Medal
Uganda Independence Medal
Malawi Independence Medal
Service Medal of the Order of St John
Badge of the Order of the League of Mercy
Voluntary Medical Service Medal
Women's Voluntary Service Medal
South African Medal for War Services
Colonial Special Constabulary Medal
OTHER COMMONWEALTH MEMBERS' ORDERS, DECORATIONS
   AND MEDALS (instituted since 1949, otherwise than by The
   Sovereign) and awards by the States of Malaysia and the
   State of Brunei.[14]
FOREIGN ORDERS (in order of date of award)[15]
FOREIGN DECORATIONS (in order of date of award)[15]
FOREIGN MEDALS (in order of date of award)[15]

* * *

*Note on Awards for Gallantry; Order of the British Empire and
British Empire Medal*

Appointments to, or promotions in, the Order of the
British Empire and awards of the British Empire Medal,
granted after 14 January 1958, for gallantry, are so described,
and a silver oak leaf Emblem is worn on the riband. When
the riband only is worn the Emblem is worn in miniature.
Classification of an award as made for gallantry has no effect
on seniority or precedence in the various Classes of the Order.
A person appointed to the Order after 14 January 1958, for
gallantry, and subsequently promoted in the Order, retains
and wears the Emblem whether promoted for gallantry or
otherwise. A holder of the British Empire Medal for Gallantry, granted since 14 January 1958, if subsequently appointed
to the Order, continues to wear the Emblem on the riband
of the Medal and wears the Emblem also on the riband of the
Order only if appointed to the Order for gallantry. On the
riband of the British Empire Medal for Gallantry, the Gallantry Emblem is worn above any Bar which may have been
granted, and when ribands are worn alone the Gallantry
Emblem is farther from the left shoulder than any silver
rose Emblem denoting the award of a Bar.

Note on Letters After the Name

All those Honours, Decorations and Medals marked ‖ in the list above entitle the holders to use the appropriate letters after the name. These groups of letters should be shown in the same order as the order of wear, subject to the following exceptions marked ‖ ‖.

The letters 'Bart.' or 'Bt.' and shown directly after the surname before all other letters after the name.

The Medal for Meritorious Service only carries a right to letters after the name if it was awarded in the Navy before 20 July 1928.

Note on Mentions in Despatches, King's Commendations and Queen's Commendations

MENTION IN DESPATCHES, 1914–19

The Emblem of bronze oak leaves denoting a Mention in Despatches during the First World War, 1914–19, is worn on the riband of the Victory Medal. The award of this Emblem ceased as from 10 August 1920.

MENTION IN DESPATCHES, 1920–39

The single bronze oak leaf Emblem, if granted for service in operations between the two World Wars, is worn on the riband of the appropriate General Service Medal. If a General Service Medal has not been granted, the Emblem is worn directly on the coat after any Medal ribands.[16]

MENTION IN DESPATCHES, 1939–45

The single bronze oak leaf Emblem signifying in the armed Forces and the Merchant Navy, either a Mention in Despatches, a King's Commendation for brave conduct, or a King's Commendation for valuable service in the air, if granted for service in the Second World War, 1939–45, is worn on the riband of the War Medal, 1939–45. If the War Medal has not been granted, the Emblem is worn directly on the coat, after any Medal ribands.[16]

MENTION IN DESPATCHES, 1945, AND SUBSEQUENTLY

The single bronze oak leaf Emblem, if granted for service in operations after the cessation of hostilities in the Second World War, is worn on the riband of the appropriate General Service or Campaign Medal. If such Medal has not been granted, the Emblem is worn directly on the coat after any Medal ribands.[16]

The single bronze oak leaf Emblem is also used in the Forces to denote a King's or Queen's Commendation for brave conduct or a King's or Queen's Commendation for valuable service in the air granted since the cessation of hostilities in the Second World War.

KING'S COMMENDATION FOR BRAVE CONDUCT 1939–45, AND SUBSEQUENTLY; QUEEN'S COMMENDATION FOR BRAVE CONDUCT, 1952, AND SUBSEQUENTLY

The Emblem of silver laurel leaves granted to civilians, other than those in the Merchant Navy, to denote a King's Commendation for brave conduct during the Second World War, 1939–45, is worn on the riband of the Defence Medal. When the Defence Medal has not been granted or the award is for services subsequent to the war, the Emblem of silver laurel leaves is worn directly on the coat after any Medal ribands.[16]

KING'S COMMENDATION FOR VALUABLE SERVICE IN THE AIR, 1939–45, AND SUBSEQUENTLY; QUEEN'S COMMENDATION FOR VALUABLE SERVICE IN THE AIR, 1952, AND SUBSEQUENTLY

The oval silver Badge granted to denote a civil King's Commendation or Queen's Commendation for valuable service in the air is worn on the coat immediately below any Medals or Medal ribands,[16] or in civil air line uniform on the panel of the left breast pocket.

*   *   *

FOOTNOTES

|| *See 'Note on letters after the name'.*

[1] *These Orders are not worn in miniature and the ribands of the Orders are not worn with Undress Uniform.*

[2] *These Orders are not worn in miniature, but are worn round the neck on all occasions except with Service Dress and certain Orders of Undress Uniform.*

[3] *This Order is not worn in miniature.*

[4] *See 'Note on awards for gallantry'.*

[5] *The Indian Order of Merit (Military and Civil) is distinct from the Order of Merit instituted in 1902.*

[6] *The Official Medal awarded previously on the recommendation of the Board of Trade, Minister of Shipping or Minister of War Transport and now on the recommendation of the Minister of Transport.*

[7] *The Indian Order of Merit (Military and Civil) is distinct from the Order of Merit instituted in 1902.*

[8] *Formerly the Medal of the Order of the British Empire for Meritorious Service; also includes the Medal of the Order awarded before 14 December 1922. See Note on awards for gallantry on page 175.*

[9] *Campaign Stars and Medals awarded for service during the First World War, 1914–19, should be worn in the following Order: 1914 Star, 1914–15 Star, British War Medal, Mercantile Marine War Medal, Victory Medal, Territorial Force War Medal, India General Service Medal (1908) (for operations in Afghanistan, 1919). Campaign Stars and Medals awarded for service in the Second World War, 1939–45, should be worn in the following order: 1939–45 Star, Atlantic Star, Air Crew Europe Star, Africa Star, Pacific Star, Burma Star, Italy Star, France and Germany Star, Defence Medal, Volunteer Service Medal of Canada, War Medal 1939–45, Africa Service Medal of the Union of South Africa, India Service Medal, New Zealand War Service Medal, Southern Rhodesia Service Medal, Australia Service Medal.*

The order of wearing of the Africa General Service Medal (1902), India General Service Medal (1908), Naval General Service Medal (1915), General Service Medal (Army and Royal Air Force) (1918) and India General Service Medal (1936) will vary and will depend upon the dates of participation in the relevant campaigns. A General Service Medal, 1962, was instituted by The Queen in 1964. A Pakistan General Service Medal was instituted by King George VI in 1951. A Sierra Leone General Service Medal, was instituted by Queen Elizabeth II, for award from 1961.

[10] *The holder of a Colonial Police Medal for Meritorious Service who is subsequently awarded a Bar to the medal for gallant conduct, should wear the Meritorious Service Medal and gallantry Bar, and the Meritorious Service riband with gallantry rose emblem in the order assigned to the Colonial Police Medal for Gallantry.*

[11] *King George V's Durbar Medal 1911, in Gold, can be worn in the United Kingdom only by those who received it as Ruling Chiefs of India.*

[12] *Formerly known as the Rocket Apparatus Volunteer Long Service Medal and awarded on the recommendation of the Board of Trade, the Minister of Shipping or Minister of War Transport, and now on the recommendation of the Minister of Transport.*

[13] *Instituted by King George VI to commemorate the constitutional change which resulted in the independence of India on 15 August 1947.*

[14] *With the exception that in the presence of the President, Ruler or Head of State of the Member country whose Government made the award, provided he is in that country, or on official occasions, in that country as may be prescribed by the Government thereof, the following full-sized insignia of Orders, viz. Collars, Shoulder Ribands, Stars and Neck Badges may be worn in front of all other awards; in either circumstances in the relative order of wear of the country whose Government made the award.*

[15] *These awards may be worn only when The Sovereign's permission has been given.*

[16] *If there are no Medal ribands, the Emblem is worn in the position in which a single riband would be worn.*

The above details have been kindly supplied by The Central Chancery of the Orders of Knighthood.

POST-NOMINAL LETTERS

THE SEVENTY-TWO SETS OF AUTHORIZED LETTERS

1 **V.C.**	29 C.V.O.	*54 I.D.S.M.
2 **G.C.**	30 C.B.E.	*55 B.G.M.
3 K.G.[1]	31 D.S.O.	56 D.S.M.
4 K.T.[1]	32 M.V.O.[4]	57 M.M.
5 K.P.	33 O.B.E.	58 D.F.M.
6 G.C.B.[2]	34 I.S.O.	59 A.F.M.
7 O.M.	M.V.O.[5]	60 S.G.M.
* 8 G.C.S.I.[3]	35 M.B.E.	* I.O.M.[14]
9 G.C.M.G.[2]	*36 I.O.M.[6]	*61 E.G.M.[15]
*10 G.C.I.E.[3]	37 O.B.[7]	62 C.P.M.[7]
*11 C.I.	38 R.R.C.	63 B.E.M.
12 G.C.V.O.[2]	39 D.S.C.	**64 C.M. or
13 G.B.E.[2]	40 M.C.	M.duC.
14 C.H.	41 D.F.C.	* K.P.M.[8]
15 K.C.B.	42 A.F.C.	* K.P.F.S.M.[8]
16 D.C.B.	43 A.R.R.C.	Q.P.M.[8]
*17 K.C.S.I.	*44 O.B.I.	Q.F.S.M.[8]
18 K.C.M.G.	O.B.[8]	C.P.M.[8]
19 D.C.M.G.	45 A.M.[9]	65 M.S.M.[16]
*20 K.C.I.E.	46 D.C.M.	66 E.R.D.[17]
21 K.C.V.O.	47 C.G.M.[10]	*67 V.D.[18]
22 D.C.V.O.	48 G.M.	68 T.D.[19]
23 K.B.E.	*49 K.P.M.[11]	69 E.D.[20]
24 D.B.E.	*50 K.P.F.S.M.[11]	70 R.D.
25 C.B.	51 Q.P.M.[12]	*71 V.R.D.
*26 C.S.I.	**52 Q.F.S.M.[12]	72 C.D.
27 C.M.G.	53 E.M.	
*28 C.I.E.	* D.C.M.[13]	

* Denotes no longer awarded but that one or more recipient survives.
** No award of this medal has yet been made.
1 Not used for Ladies of the Order of the Garter or of the Thistle.
2 Used also by Dames Grand Cross.
3 Used also by Dames Grand Commander.

4 When of the 4th Class.
5 When of the 5th Class.
6 When in the Military Division.
7 When for Gallantry.
8 When for Distinguished or Good Service.
9 Medals in Gold no longer awarded; Albert Medal now only awarded posthumously.
10 Used both for the naval medal and for the flying medal.
11 When for Gallantry.
12 When for Gallantry; posthumous only.
13 If for Royal West African Frontier Force or the King's African Rifles.
14 When in the Civil Division.
15 Now usable only in reference to unexchangeable honorary awards before the creation of the George Cross in 1940.
16 Post nominal letters used by custom only if awarded for naval service before 20th July 1928.
17 Emergency Reserve Decoration (Army).
18 Denotes the Volunteer Officers' Decoration (1892–1908); V.D. for India and the Colonies (1894–1930), and the Colonial Auxiliary Forces Officers' Decoration (1899–1930).
19 Denotes both the T.D. (1908–30), the Efficiency Decoration (instituted 1930) if awarded to an officer of the (Home) Auxiliary Military Forces, and the T.A.V.R. Decoration (instituted 1969).
20 Denotes the Efficiency Decoration when awarded to an officer of Commonwealth or Colonial Auxiliary Forces.

Note that the post-nominal letters G.M.B., G.M.S.I., G.M.M.G., G.M.I.E., G.M.V.O. and G.M.B.E., indicating the Great Master of the Order of the Bath, and Grand Masters of the Orders of the Star of India, St Michael and St George, Indian Empire, Victorian Order and British Empire, though used, are not officially authorized.

Decorations which do not carry authorized post-nominal letters are:
1 Royal Victorian Chain.
2 Royal Order of Victoria and Albert[1].
3 Kaiser-i-Hind Medal next after the O.B.I.
4 Order of St John next after the Order of Burma (for good service).

5 Union of South Africa King's (or Queen's) Medal for Bravery in Gold, next after the A.M.

6 Union of South Africa King's (or Queen's) Medal for Bravery in Silver, next after the B.G.M.

7 Constabulary Medal (Ireland).

8 9, 10 and 11, India, Burma, Ceylon and Sierra Leone Police Medals for Gallantry, in that order next after the E.G.M.

12 Sierra Leone Fire Brigade Medal for Gallantry, next after the Sierra Leone Police Medal for Gallantry.

13 Uganda Services Medal (if for Gallantry), next after the Colonial Police Medal for Gallantry.

14 Life Saving Medal of the Order of St John, next after the Canada Medal.

15 Royal Victorian Medal (in Gold, Silver or Bronze), next after Polar Medals.

16 Imperial Service Medal, next after the Royal Victorian Medal.

17 Police Medals for Meritorious Service (other than King's/Queen's medals), next after the Imperial Services Medal.

18 Uganda Services Medal (if for meritorious service), next after Police Medals above.

[1]*Widely denoted however as V.A. in quasi-official references.*

The following post-nominal letters were previously used:

K.B.	indicated Knighthood of the Order of the Bath prior to its division into three classes in 1815.
G.C.H., K.C.H. and K.H.	indicated membership of one of the three classes – Knights Grand Cross, Knights Commander or Knights – of 'The Order of the Guelphs' conferred from 1815 to 1837 during the Union of the Crowns of Hanover and the United Kingdom.
K.S.I.	Knights of the Most Excellent Order of the Star of India. This designation was used between 1861 and 1866 before the Order was enlarged into three classes.
C.S.C.	Conspicuous Service Cross (instituted in 1901); redesignated D.S.C. in 1914.

(with amendments added)

The above details have been extracted by permission from 'British Gallantry Awards' published by Guinness Superlatives Ltd.

GLOSSARY

bars   These are the additions to the medal with the names of the campaigns or service thereon.   In a few cases, the bars are affixed to the ribbon, and not to the piece; an example of this is the bar for the 1914 Star.

clasp   This is an alternative term for bar, though sometimes used to designate the suspender.

claw   This is the fitting on the piece which joins it to the suspender.

coinage head   This is the Sovereign's head as used on coins. In the case of service medals it is generally crowned when used in the reign of King George VI.

ears   These are the fittings at both ends of the bars to enable subsequent bars to be fitted; in many cases they are hidden by roses.

edge   The outside circumference of the piece which usually bears the recipient's name, and particulars.

embossed   This means that the wording or matters referred to is raised, such as the recipient's name on the reverse of the Abyssinian Medals issued to Europeans.

engraved   This means that the inscription of such matter as is found on the edge, such as the particulars of the recipient, is engraved.

exergue   The space below the horizontal line on the reverse

group   A group of medals are those awarded to one recipient.

impressed   This means that the particulars on the edge have been impressed.

indented   This means that the particulars on the edge have been indented.

obverse   The side of the piece which usually bears the Sovereign's head.   There are, however, many medals which bear other heads, such as those awarded for Waterloo, the Sarawak Long Service Medal and others.

reverse The opposite to observe. This generally bears a design or inscription, and sometimes both.

rim The raised part of the edge which prevents damage to the piece when it is laid flat.

INDEX

The figures in **bold type** *refer to the medal numbers in the text margins, not to page numbers*